DIBELS® Next

Assessment Manual

Roland H. Good III and Ruth A. Kaminski

with: Kelli Cummings, Chantal Dufour-Martel, Kathleen Petersen, Kelly Powell-Smith, Stephanie Stollar, and Joshua Wallin

www.sooprislearning.com/DIBELS

4 5 6 7 8 BNG 16 15 14 13 12

ISBN 13: 978-1-60697-359-2
ISBN 10: 1-60697-359-2

272911/354/02-12

Printed in the United States of America

Published and Distributed by

4093 Specialty Place • Longmont, Colorado 80504
(303) 651-2829 • www.soprislearning.com

Welcome to DIBELS® *Next*

Powerful Indicators for Improving Student Outcomes

Over the last decade, *DIBELS* (*Dynamic Indicators of Basic Early Literacy Skills*) has changed the educational landscape—providing accurate, timely benchmark and progress monitoring information to ensure students receive targeted instructional support. This premier universal assessment system has been embraced by educators across the country and used as a tool to help thousands of students reach their full academic potential.

What is *DIBELS Next*?

DIBELS Next represents a **breakthrough revision**, based on new research conducted over four years on more than 25,000 students in 90 schools throughout the United States, as well as consumer feedback. *DIBELS Next* retains the best of *DIBELS* but has been updated to increase ease of use and accuracy of results.

DIBELS Next measures are **brief, powerful indicators** of foundational early literacy skills that:

- are **quick** and **efficient** to administer and score;
- serve as **universal screening** (or **benchmark assessment**) and **progress monitoring**;
- identify students in need of **intervention support**;
- evaluate the **effectiveness of interventions**; and
- support the **RtI/Multitiered model**.

What are the significant changes in *DIBELS Next*?

- **First Sound Fluency** replaces Initial Sound Fluency as an easy-to-administer, reliable measure of early phonemic awareness.
- **Daze**, a new comprehension measure based on maze procedures, has been added for grades 3 through 6.
- All new ***DIBELS*** **Oral Reading Fluency** passages that have been field-tested with students and are empirically leveled.
- Revised **Nonsense Word Fluency** measures the alphabetic principle and foundational phonics, with new directions and scoring rules to include the number of whole words read correctly.

Other new features include:

- more **clear and concise directions** and **scoring rules**;
- **new arrangement of items** to increase reliability of scores;
- checklists of **common response patterns** to facilitate targeted instruction;
- **new reliability and validity data** on all measures, including correlations between *DIBELS* Oral Reading Fluency and a NAEP reading fluency passage; and
- new **user-friendly format**.

This *DIBELS Next Assessment Manual* provides:

- an overview of how *DIBELS Next* measures align with basic early literacy skills;
- general guidelines on the administration and scoring of the *DIBELS Next* measures, and how to interpret results;
- specific administration and scoring procedures for each measure; and
- a pronunciation guide, practice scoring sheets and answer keys, assessment accuracy checklists, and sample statements and parent letters.

Anyone who administers *DIBELS Next* or uses *DIBELS Next* scores should read this manual. The best understanding of the information in this manual will come after the reader attends training that includes practice in administering and scoring each *DIBELS Next* measure. Training in how to interpret the data is also important for the reader who will be interpreting the test results or using those results to make group- or student-level decisions. For more information about training, see page 22.

Table of Contents

Acknowledgments viii

Chapter 1: Introduction to *DIBELS Next* 1

The Basic Early Literacy Skills 1

An Overview of the *DIBELS Next* Measures 2

DIBELS Next and the Basic Early Literacy Skills 2

DIBELS and Students With Special Needs 5

How *DIBELS Next* Is Used 6

DIBELS Next and RtI: The Outcomes-Driven Model 8

History and Development of *DIBELS Next* 10

Transitioning to *DIBELS Next* 10

Chapter 2: Guidelines for Administering and Scoring *DIBELS Next* 15

Standard Features of *DIBELS Next* Measures 15

Administration Guidelines 16

General Scoring Guidelines 18

Testing Materials 19

Accommodations 21

Training 22

Appropriate Test Use of *DIBELS* 23

Test Security 23

Chapter 3: Interpreting *DIBELS Next* Data 25

Criterion-Referenced Interpretations: Understanding Benchmark Goals and Cut Points for Risk 25

Individually Referenced Interpretations: Analyzing Student Growth and Progress Over Time 27

Local Norm-Referenced Interpretations: Comparing Students Districtwide 28

Systemwide or National Norm-Referenced Interpretations: Comparing Students in a Larger Context 29

The Importance of Response Patterns 30

Chapter 4: Implementing *DIBELS Next* in Your School 31

Conducting Benchmark Assessment 31

Conducting Progress Monitoring 37

Communicating With Students, Parents, and School Personnel 41

Chapter 5: *DIBELS* First Sound Fluency (FSF) 43

Overview 43

Administration Directions 44

Scoring Rules 46

Chapter 6: *DIBELS* Letter Naming Fluency (LNF) 53

Overview 53

Administration Directions 54

Scoring Rules 55

Chapter 7: *DIBELS* Phoneme Segmentation Fluency (PSF) 61

Overview 61

Administration Directions 62

Scoring Rules 63

Chapter 8: *DIBELS* Nonsense Word Fluency (NWF) 73

Overview 73

Administration Directions 75

Scoring Rules 76

Chapter 9: *DIBELS* Oral Reading Fluency (DORF) 87

Overview 87

Administration Directions 88

Scoring Rules for DORF 91

Scoring Rules for Retell 98

Chapter 10: Daze 109

Overview 109

Administration Directions 110

Scoring Rules 111

Appendices 113

Appendix 1: Pronunciation Guide 115

Appendix 2: Practice Scoring Sheets and Answer Keys 117

Appendix 3: Assessment Accuracy Checklists 125

Appendix 4: Sample Statement and Letters 133

Appendix 5: Benchmark Goals and Cut Points for Risk 137

Appendix 6: *DIBELS* Composite Score 147

Bibliography 155

Acknowledgments

The program of research and development that has culminated in *DIBELS Next* has been a collaborative effort among many dedicated contributors. The talents and efforts of literally thousands of individuals contributed to the successful completion of this edition of *Dynamic Indicators of Basic Early Literacy Skills*, including Dynamic Measurement Group research scientists and staff, research colleagues from across the country, educators and school personnel, children and parents, and publishing partners.

Throughout a four-year program of research and focused effort, these individuals provided skill, expertise, time, and unlimited energy for the research and development of *DIBELS Next*. Listings of those people who contributed to the research and development of *DIBELS Next* are included in this manual and in the Technical Manual. There are, in addition, numerous unnamed children, teachers, and school personnel to whom we owe our special thanks. These people volunteered their time to participate in the research and provided invaluable feedback and suggestions on the measures. We are deeply indebted to each and every individual for his or her contribution.

Ruth Kaminski and Roland H. Good, III

February, 2010

Research Scientists

Kelli Cummings, Ph.D.
Chantal Dufour-Martel, Ph.D.
Nancy Knutson, Ph.D.
Kathleen Petersen, Ph.D.
Kelly Powell-Smith, Ph.D.
Stephanie Stollar, Ph.D.

Project Manager

Joshua Wallin

Graphic Designer

Karla Wysocki

Research Assistants

Alisa Dorman
Rebecca Freund
Annie Hommel
Douglas Rice
Katherine Bravo Aguayo

Data Analysis Team

Elizabeth Dewey
Rachael Latimer
Maya O'Neil

Support Staff

Daniel Cohn
Laura Collins
Carol Gassman
Jeff Heriot
Sarah Laszlo

Field Site Coordinators

Ann Marie Anderson
Theresa Fletcher
Lana Gerber
Mary Giboney
Allison Hardin
Debra Hawkins
Tammy Hillebrand
Carol Keskeny
Sara Krebs
Kristen MacConnell
Tina McMullen
Amy Murdoch
Kristin Orton
Lori Pinchot
Alecia Rahn-Blakeslee
Karla Reed
Janet Reynolds
Janet Richards
Christina Schmid
Sue Spiker
Lisa Habedank Stewart
Peggy Taylor
Carol Trumbo
Lillian Vardon
Jennifer Watson-Kilgrow
Christi Whitter

Chapter 1: **Introduction to *DIBELS Next***

Dynamic Indicators of Basic Early Literacy Skills (DIBELS) is a set of measures used to assess early literacy and reading skills for students from kindergarten through sixth grade. You can use *DIBELS Next* to:

- identify students who may be at risk for reading difficulties;
- help teachers identify areas to target instructional support;
- monitor at-risk students while they receive additional, targeted instruction; and
- examine the effectiveness of your school's system of instructional supports.

DIBELS is designed to be an efficient, cost-effective tool to help make decisions about reading instruction, to help the teacher provide support early, and to prevent the occurrence of later reading difficulties. *DIBELS* assesses *basic early literacy skills*, or the essential skills that every child must master to become a proficient reader (National Reading Panel, 2000; National Research Council, 1998).

The Basic Early Literacy Skills

- ***Phonemic Awareness:*** Hearing and using sounds in spoken words.
- ***Phonics:*** The system of letter-sound relationships that serves as the foundation for decoding words in print.
  - *Alphabetic Principle and Basic Phonics:* The concept that printed letters correspond to the sounds of spoken words. Knowing the most common sounds of consonants and vowels and sounding out phonetically regular VC and CVC words.
  - *Advanced Phonics and Word Attack Skills:* Knowing all of the sounds for letters and letter combinations, and sounding out written words.
- ***Accurate and Fluent Reading of Connected Text:*** Reading stories and passages easily and confidently with few mistakes.
- ***Reading Comprehension:*** Understanding what is read.
- ***Vocabulary and Language Skills:*** Understanding and correctly using a variety of words.

An Overview of the *DIBELS Next* Measures

DIBELS Next comprises six measures.

1. ***First Sound Fluency (FSF):*** The assessor says words, and the student says the first sound for each word.
2. ***Letter Naming Fluency (LNF):*** The student is presented with a sheet of letters and asked to name the letters.
3. ***Phoneme Segmentation Fluency (PSF):*** The assessor says words, and the student says the individual sounds in each word.
4. ***Nonsense Word Fluency (NWF):*** The student is presented with a list of VC and CVC nonsense words (e.g., sig, rav, ov) and asked to read the words.
5. **DIBELS *Oral Reading Fluency (DORF):*** The student is presented with a reading passage and asked to read aloud. The student is then asked to retell what he/she just read.
6. ***Daze:*** The student is presented with a reading passage in which some words are replaced by a multiple choice box that includes the original word and two distractors. The student reads the passage silently and selects the word in each box that best fits the meaning of the sentence.

The *DIBELS Next* measures were designed to be economical and efficient indicators of a student's basic early literacy skills, and include the following features:

- They are *standardized assessments*, which means they are administered and scored exactly the same way every time with every student. An assessment must be standardized in order to be able to compare results across students or across time, or to compare student scores to a target goal.
- They include alternate forms of approximately equal difficulty so that student progress can be measured over time.
- They are brief so that students can be assessed efficiently and frequently.
- They are reliable, which means they provide a relatively stable assessment of the skill across time, different forms, and different assessors.
- They are valid, which means they are measuring the essential early literacy skills they are intended to measure.
- They are sensitive to student growth over relatively short periods of time.

DIBELS Next and the Basic Early Literacy Skills

Assessing student performance on the basic early literacy skills, which are also known as *core components* or *foundational skills*, can help distinguish children who are on track to become successful readers from children who are likely to struggle. Evidence shows that these skills are the basic building blocks that every child must master in order to become a proficient reader (Adams, 1990; National Reading Panel, 2000; National Research Council, 1998). Evidence also shows that these skills can be improved with instruction (Kame'enui, Carnine, Dixon, Simmons, & Coyne, 2002; Simmons & Kame'enui, 1998; Torgesen et al., 1999).

The *DIBELS Next* measures are designed to be *indicators* of the basic early literacy skills. An indicator is a brief, efficient index that provides a fair degree of certainty about a larger, more complex system or process. For example, a pediatrician measures a child's height and weight as a quick and efficient indicator of that child's physical development. Similarly, each *DIBELS Next* measure is a quick and efficient indicator of how well a child is doing in learning a particular basic early literacy skill (see *Table 1.1*). As indicators, *DIBELS* measures are not intended to be comprehensive, in-depth assessments of each and every component of a basic early literacy skill. Instead, they are designed to measure key components that are representative of that skill area, and predictive of overall reading competence.

Table 1.1 Alignment of *DIBELS Next* Measures With Basic Early Literacy Skills

Basic Early Literacy Skills	*DIBELS* Indicators
Phonemic Awareness	First Sound Fluency (FSF) Phoneme Segmentation Fluency (PSF)
Alphabetic Principle and Basic Phonics	Nonsense Word Fluency (NWF) –Correct Letter Sounds –Whole Words Read
Advanced Phonics and Word Attack Skills	*DIBELS* Oral Reading Fluency (DORF) –Accuracy
Accurate and Fluent Reading of Connected Text	*DIBELS* Oral Reading Fluency (DORF) –Correct Words Per Minute –Accuracy
Reading Comprehension	Daze *DIBELS* Oral Reading Fluency (DORF) –Correct Words Per Minute –Retell Total/Quality of Response
Vocabulary and Language Skills	Word Use Fluency-Revised (WUF-R) (available as an experimental measure from http://dibels.org/)

Letter Naming Fluency (LNF) is an indicator of risk that is not directly linked to any of the basic early literacy skills. *DIBELS* Oral Reading Fluency (DORF) is a complex measure that represents many different skills. In addition to measuring the accurate and fluent reading of connected text, DORF also looks at advanced phonics and word attack skills by examining the student's accuracy. DORF is a good indicator of reading comprehension for most students, and the retell component helps to identify the small number of students for whom DORF may not be a good indicator of comprehension. DORF and Daze also require adequate vocabulary and language to comprehend the content of the passages.

The model in *Figure 1.1* (next page) shows the relationships among the basic early literacy skills, the *DIBELS Next* measures, and the timeline for achieving benchmark goals for each measure. The basic early literacy skills (e.g., phonemic awareness, phonics) are represented by the rounded boxes at the top of the figure. The arrows connecting the rounded boxes show how the early literacy skills relate to one another and lead to reading comprehension. The arrows from the rounded boxes to the boxes in the middle level show the linkage between the basic early literacy skills and the *DIBELS Next* measures. The lines between the

Figure 1.1 Model of Basic Early Literacy Skills, *DIBELS* Indicators, and Timeline

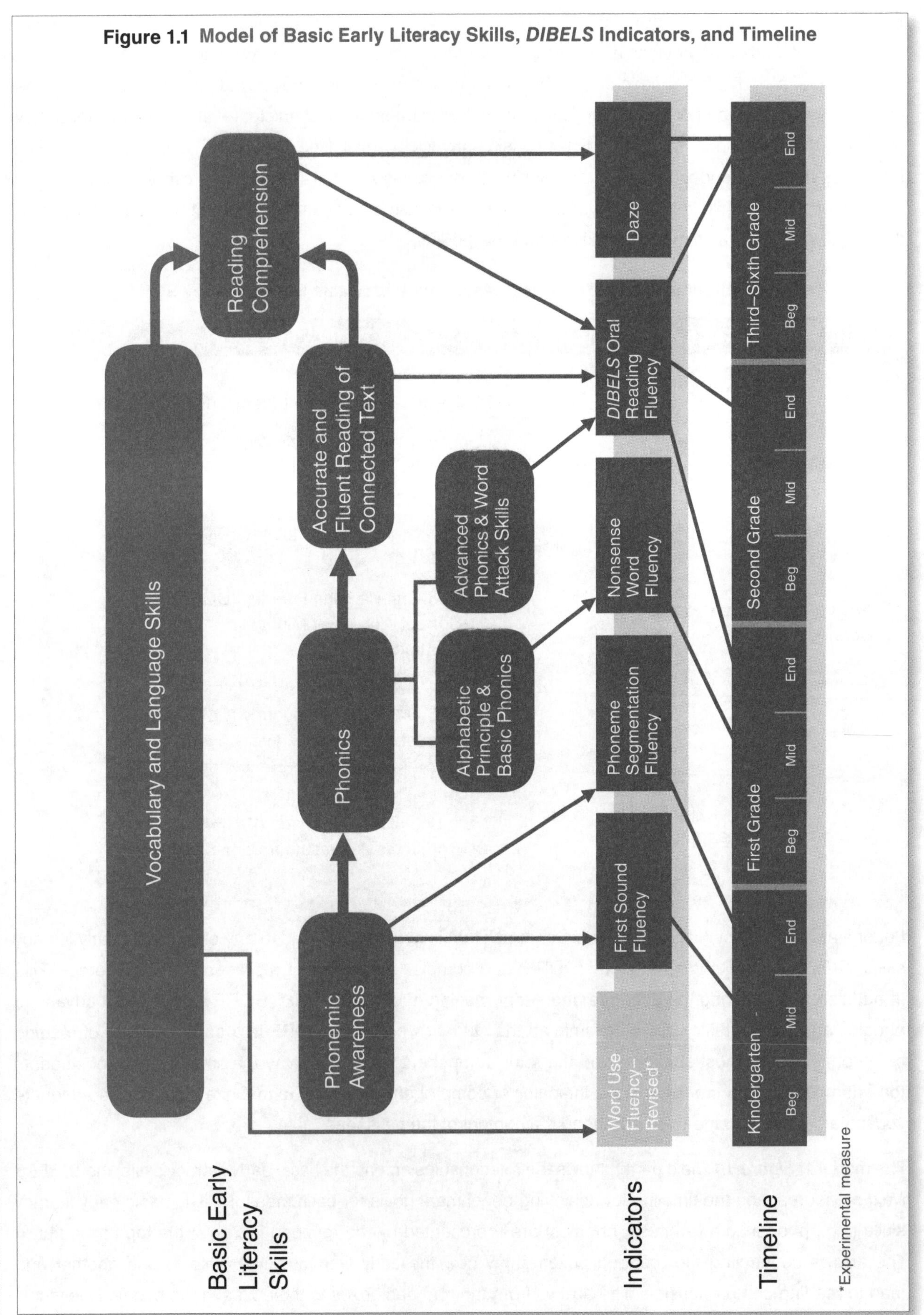

DIBELS Next measures and the timeline at the bottom indicate the target time of the benchmark goals for that measure. In this model, *automaticity with the code* (i.e., accurate and fluent reading of connected text) in combination with *vocabulary and language skills* provide a necessary foundation for learning reading comprehension skills. If the student does not have adequate skills in either area, the development of reading comprehension skills is likely to be compromised.

The model is intended to highlight the primary, most powerful, and instructionally relevant relationships. Other, secondary relationships between core components are not included in this figure for clarity. For example, in addition to the relationship between phonemic awareness and phonics, there is also a reciprocal relationship between phonics and phonemic awareness. The model emphasizes this set of relationships in a prevention-oriented framework in which phonemic awareness skills can be developed very early and can provide a foundation for successful phonics instruction.

Two caveats are important to note with respect to *Figure 1.1.* First, the figure is intended to assist in organizing the developmental progression of skills and the linkage to the *DIBELS Next* indicators and timeline. Although the core components are portrayed as distinct rounded boxes, the skills are tightly intertwined in proficient reading. Phonemic awareness and phonics skills, for example, might be taught and practiced in isolation in a designed curriculum, but instruction is not complete until the skills are integrated. A complete understanding of how words are portrayed in written English requires the integration of all core components into a coherent whole. Second, the role of systematic and explicit instruction is critical throughout this model. Acquisition and mastery of an earlier skill by itself is unlikely to result in achievement of the subsequent skill. However, a foundation of an earlier-developed skill combined with systematic and explicit instruction in the subsequent skill is likely to result in successful achievement.

DIBELS and Students With Special Needs

DIBELS is appropriate for most students for whom an instructional goal is to learn to read in English. For English language learners who are learning to read in English, *DIBELS* is appropriate for assessing and monitoring progress in acquisition of early reading skills. *DIBELS* has been used successfully with English language learners (e.g., Haager & Windmueller, 2001). In addition, research findings indicate that children who are English language learners can learn to read as well in English as their English-speaking peers (Chiappe, Siegel, & Wade-Woolley, 2002; Geva, Yaghoub-Zadeh, & Schuster, 2000) and, in fact, often outperform their peers in phonemic skills (Lesaux & Siegel, 2003).

DIBELS is also appropriate for students in special education for whom learning to read connected text is an IEP goal. For students receiving special education, it may be necessary to adjust goals and timelines and use below-grade materials for progress monitoring.

There are a few groups of students for whom *DIBELS* is not appropriate: (a) students who are learning to read in a language other than English; (b) students who are deaf; (c) students who have fluency-based speech disabilities such as stuttering and oral apraxia; and (d) students with severe disabilities for whom learning to read connected text is not an IEP goal.

Students who are learning to read in a language other than English. *DIBELS* is designed to provide information about the progress of children in acquiring literacy skills for reading in English. For children who are learning to read in languages other than English, it would be most meaningful and appropriate to assess their acquisition of reading skills in the language in which they are being instructed. For example, students learning to read in Spanish might be assessed using the Spanish version of *DIBELS*, *IDEL* (*Indicadores Dinámicos del Éxito en la Lectura*).

Students who are deaf. *DIBELS* was developed based on the research examining the process of learning to read for students with functional hearing. For most students who are deaf, the ability to use phonological representations of letters is seriously compromised (Leybaert & Charlier, 1996; Moores, 1996); therefore, the core competencies assessed by *DIBELS*—phonemic awareness and phonics—may not apply or may apply differently for students who are deaf and are learning to read. *DIBELS* would be appropriate for children with mild to moderate hearing impairments who have residual hearing and who are learning phonemic awareness and phonics skills.

Students who have fluency or oral motor speech disabilities. Speech fluency is compromised in students who stutter or have oral motor speech disabilities such as oral apraxia. Given that the nature of such disabilities is slow and/or dysfluent speech (Paul, 2001), the use of fluency-based measures for these students would not be appropriate. A professional judgment is necessary for students who stutter. *DIBELS* may be appropriate for a student who stutters if the student does not stutter while reading the *DIBELS* passages or completing other *DIBELS* activities.

Students with severe disabilities. There is a small number of students for whom learning to read connected text is not an IEP goal. For these students, it would be most meaningful and appropriate to use other assessment strategies to monitor progress toward their individual IEP goals and objectives.

How *DIBELS Next* Is Used

Benchmark Assessment

Benchmark assessment refers to testing all students within a school or grade three times per year for the purpose of identifying those who may be at risk for reading difficulties. Benchmark assessment is always conducted using grade-level material. The measures administered for benchmark assessment vary by grade and time of year, and include those measures that are most relevant for making instructional decisions at that time.

Progress Monitoring

Progress monitoring refers to testing students more frequently who may be at risk for future reading difficulty on the skill areas in which they are receiving instruction, to ensure that they are making adequate progress. Progress monitoring can be conducted using grade-level or out-of-grade materials, depending on the student's needs. Decisions about the skill areas and levels to monitor are made at the individual student level.

Benchmark assessment and progress monitoring are the types of assessment necessary for use within a *Response-to-Intervention (RtI) model* such as the *Outcomes-Driven Model*. For more information on benchmark assessment and progress monitoring, see *Chapter 4: Implementing* DIBELS Next *in Your School*, page 31.

The *DIBELS Next* Benchmark Administration Timeline (*Figure 1.2*) shows the measures that are administered at each benchmark assessment period.

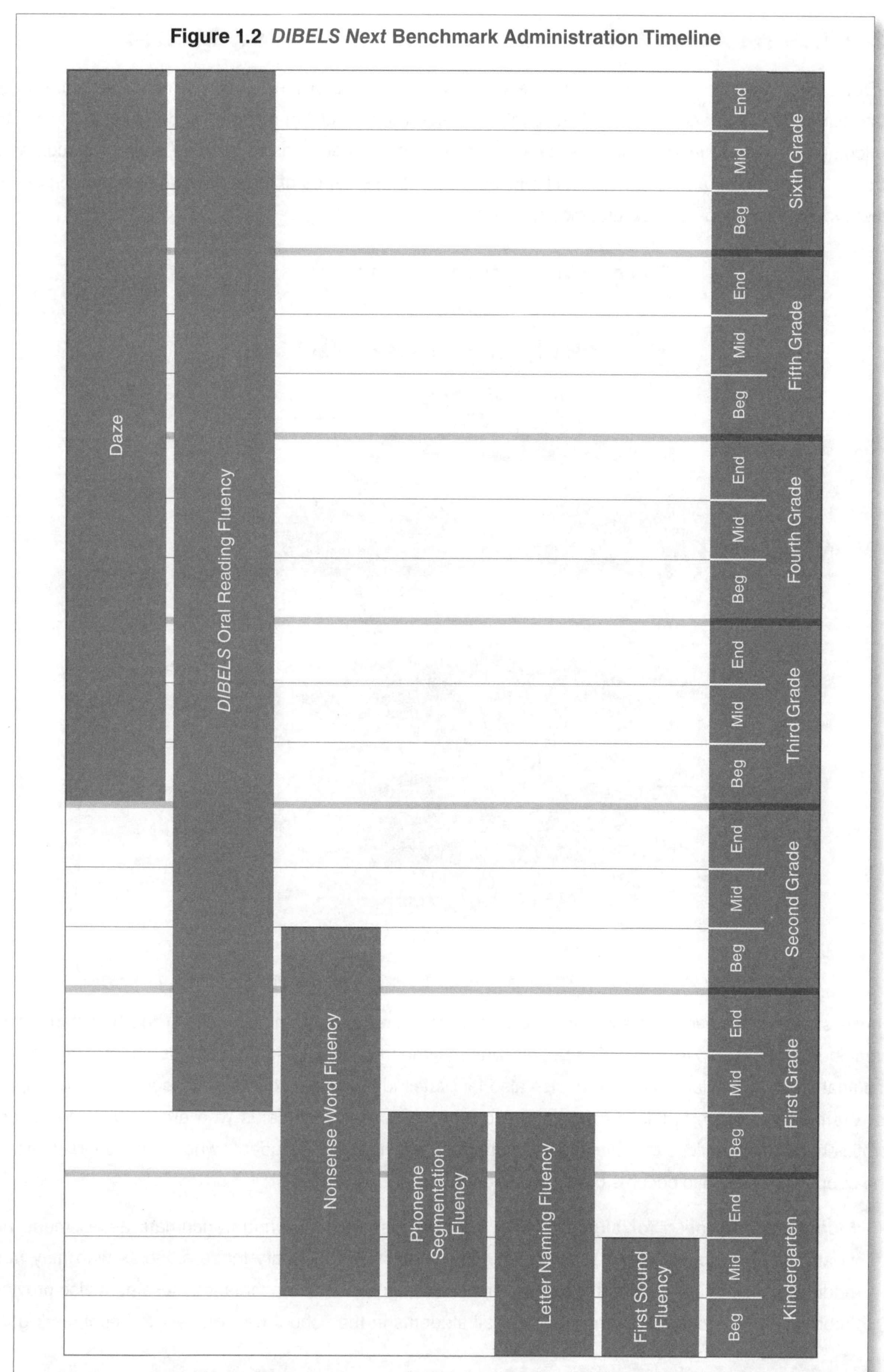

Figure 1.2 ***DIBELS Next*** **Benchmark Administration Timeline**

DIBELS Next and RtI: The Outcomes-Driven Model

DIBELS Next was developed to provide teachers with information they need to make decisions about instruction. The authors of *DIBELS* advocate a data-based decision-making model referred to as the Outcomes-Driven Model, because the data are used to make decisions to improve student outcomes by matching the amount and type of instructional support with the needs of the individual students. *Figure 1.3* illustrates the five steps of the Outcomes-Driven Model.

Figure 1.3 The Outcomes-Driven Model

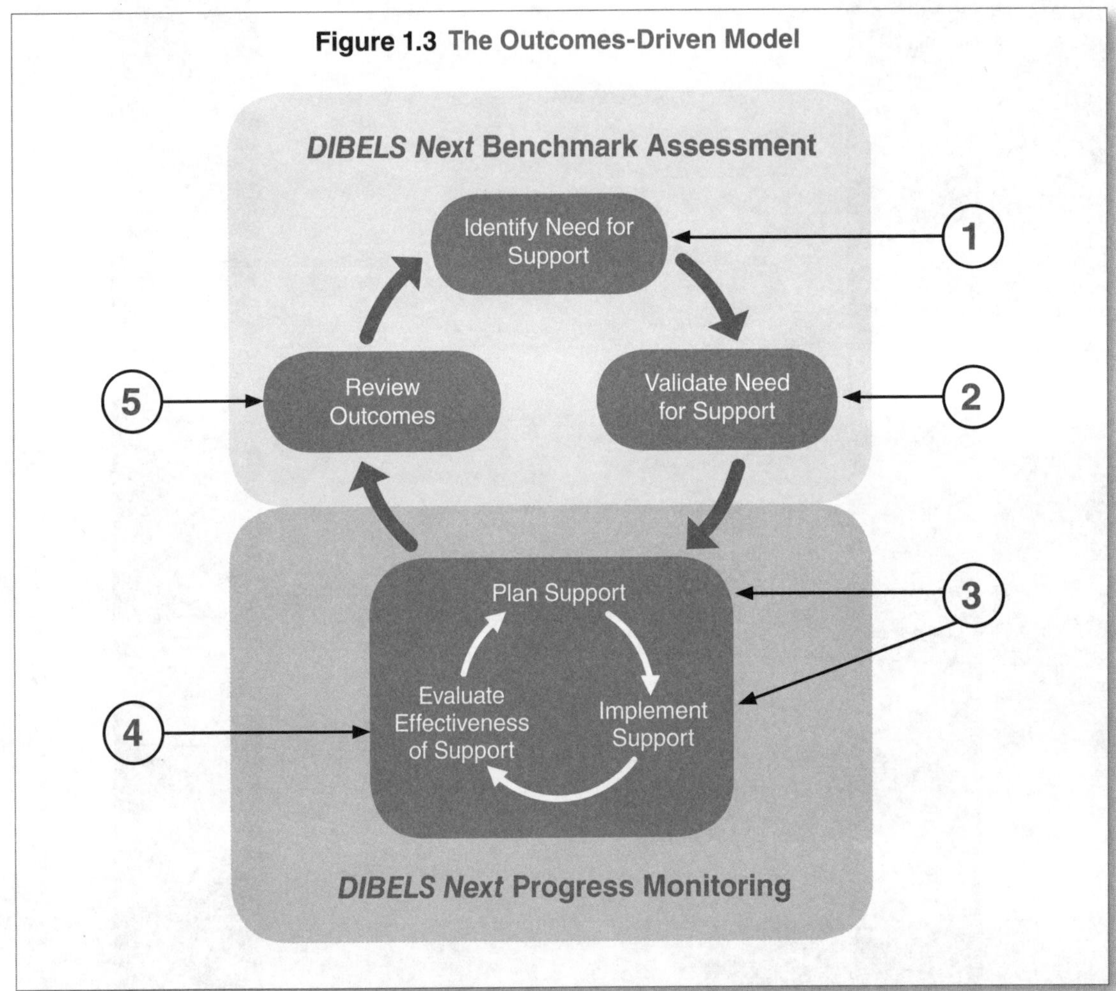

These steps repeat each semester as a student progresses through the grades. At the beginning of the semester, the first step is to identify students who may need additional support. At the end of the semester, the final step is to review outcomes, which also facilitates identifying students who need additional support for the next semester. In this manner, educators can ensure that students who are on track to become proficient readers continue to make adequate progress, and that those students who are not on track receive the support they need to become proficient readers.

Step 1: Identify need for support early. This process occurs during benchmark assessment, and is also referred to as *universal screening*. The purpose is to identify those students who may need additional instructional support to achieve benchmark goals. The benchmark assessment also provides information regarding the performance of all students in the school with respect to benchmark goals.

All students within a school or grade are tested on *DIBELS* three times per year on grade-level material. The testing occurs at the beginning, middle, and end of the school year.

Step 2: Validate need for support. The purpose of this step is to be reasonably confident that the student needs or does not need additional instructional support. Before making individual student decisions, it is important to consider additional information beyond the initial data obtained during benchmark testing. Teachers can always use additional assessment information and knowledge about a student to validate a score before making decisions about instructional support. If there is a discrepancy in the student's performance relative to other information available about the student, or if there is a question about the accuracy of a score, the score can be validated by retesting the student using alternate forms of the *DIBELS* measures or additional diagnostic assessments as necessary.

Step 3: Plan and implement support. In general, for students who are meeting the benchmark goals, a good, research-based core classroom curriculum should meet their instructional needs, and they will continue to receive benchmark assessment three times per year to ensure they remain on track. Students who are identified as needing support are likely to require additional instruction or intervention in the skill areas where they are having difficulties.

Step 4: Evaluate and modify support as needed. Students who are receiving additional support should be progress monitored more frequently to ensure that the instructional support being provided is helping them get back on track. Students should be monitored on the measures that test the skill areas where they are having difficulties and receiving additional instructional support. Monitoring may occur once per month, once every two weeks, or as often as once per week. In general, students who need the most intensive instruction are progress monitored most frequently.

Step 5: Review outcomes. By looking at the benchmark assessment data for all students, schools can ensure that their instructional supports—both core curriculum and additional interventions—are working for all students. If a school identifies areas of instructional support that are not working as desired, the school can use the data to help make decisions on how to improve.

The use of *DIBELS* within the Outcomes-Driven Model is consistent with the most recent reauthorization of the Individuals with Disabilities Education Improvement Act (IDEA), which allows the use of a Response to Intervention (RtI) approach to identify children with learning disabilities. In an RtI approach to identification, early intervention is provided to students who are at risk for the development of learning difficulties. Data are gathered to determine which students are responsive to the intervention provided and which students are in need of more intensive support (Fuchs & Fuchs, 2006). The Outcomes-Driven Model described in *Figure 1.3* is based on foundational work with a problem-solving model (see Deno, 1989; Shinn, 1995; Tilly, 2008) and the initial application of the problem-solving model to early literacy skills (Kaminski & Good, 1998). The general questions addressed by a problem-solving model include: *What is the problem? Why is it happening? What should be done about it? Did it work?* (Tilly, 2008). The Outcomes-Driven Model was developed to address these questions, but within a prevention-oriented framework designed to preempt early reading difficulty and ensure step-by-step progress toward outcomes that will result in established, adequate reading achievement.

History and Development of *DIBELS Next*

Initial research and development of *DIBELS* were conducted in the late 1980s and early 1990s. The *DIBELS* program of research builds on measurement procedures from Curriculum-Based Measurement, or CBM (e.g., Deno & Mirkin, 1977; Deno, 1985; Deno & Fuchs, 1987), and General Outcome Measurement, or GOM (Fuchs & Deno, 1991). The *DIBELS* measures were designed to be economical and efficient indicators of a student's progress toward achieving a general outcome such as reading or phonemic awareness, and to be used for both benchmark assessment and progress monitoring.

Initial research on *DIBELS* focused on examining the technical adequacy of the measures for these primary purposes (Good & Kaminski, 1996; Kaminski & Good, 1996). Since its initial publication in 2002, *DIBELS* has gained widespread use for monitoring progress in acquisition of early literacy skills. Prior to 2002, *DIBELS* was made available to research partners. An ongoing program of research over the past two decades has continued to document the reliability and validity of *DIBELS* as well as its sensitivity in measuring changes in student performance over time.

DIBELS Next is the result of an expanding knowledge base in the fields of reading and assessment, continuing research and development, and feedback from users of *DIBELS*. From 2006 to 2010, *DIBELS Next* was researched and field-tested in 90 schools across the United States. A series of studies over that time period examined the reliability, validity, and utility of the measures. See the *DIBELS Next Technical Manual* (available January, 2011, from http://dibels.org/) for a description of the technical adequacy data on *DIBELS Next* and a summary of the technical adequacy data on earlier versions.

Transitioning to *DIBELS Next*

For those who have been using *DIBELS* 6th Edition, the transition to *DIBELS Next* should not be difficult. It is suggested that the following steps be taken to ensure full understanding and fidelity of implementation of *DIBELS Next*:

> ***Step 1:*** Attend a *DIBELS Next* Transition Workshop. See page 22 for more information about training options.
>
> ***Step 2:*** Carefully read through this entire *DIBELS Next Assessment Manual*, paying particular attention to Chapters 5–10, which outline administration and scoring directions for each measure.
>
> ***Step 3:*** Practice the administration and scoring of each measure before conducting actual student assessment. All of the measures have new directions, new reminders, and new scoring rules.

What's New in *DIBELS Next*?

New content. All of the passages and forms are new. All of the content has undergone extensive review and analysis.

New and improved materials. Testing materials have been revised for improved ease of use. Measures are easier to administer and score, and wait rules, discontinue rules, and reminder prompts have been embedded into the administration directions. Scoring booklets have been made larger, and an early-reader font is used for kindergarten through second-grade materials.

New and improved directions. All of the directions that are read to the student and the reminder prompts have been revised and made more explicit to facilitate student understanding of the task.

Stratification. A stratified random sampling procedure was used to improve the equivalence of the forms and to more evenly distribute items of different difficulty. This procedure increases the consistency of scores from one form to another. With stratified random sampling, items of similar difficulty appear in the same places on every form. For example, on NWF there were six difficulty/word-type categories that were distributed by design identically on each form. For instance, the first item is always an easier item, a word with a three-letter CVC pattern where both consonants occur frequently in English. For each form, the actual test items were then randomly selected from the appropriate category.

Response patterns. Measures include lists of common response patterns that the assessor can mark to help in planning instruction. These lists are located within the scoring booklets for better accessibility.

Table 1.2 below describes the two new *DIBELS Next* measures.

Table 1.2 New *DIBELS Next* Measures

Measures	Description
First Sound Fluency (FSF)	• A new measure that replaces Initial Sound Fluency. FSF is easier to administer and eliminates the issues with ISF that were caused by the pictures, students guessing at the answers, and the assessor starting and stopping the stopwatch for each item. FSF includes production items with continuous timing. • Stratification of test items based on whether the word begins with a continuous sound, a stop sound, or a blend.
Daze	• A new measure, based on maze procedures, that has been added as an additional indicator of comprehension in grades 3 through 6. • Can be administered in groups or individually.

Table 1.3 summarizes the changes for the existing *DIBELS* measures.

Table 1.3 Summary of Changes to Existing *DIBELS* Measures

Measures	Changes
Letter Naming Fluency (LNF)	• All new forms. • New and improved materials with integrated reminders to enhance the administration of the measure. • New font that may be more familiar to younger children. • Stratification of test items to increase equivalence and consistency of scores from one form to another. • New, more explicit directions and reminders to facilitate student understanding of the task. • A checklist of common response patterns to facilitate linkages to instruction.
Phoneme Segmentation Fluency (PSF)	• All new forms. • New and improved materials with integrated reminders to enhance the administration of the measure. • New layout to facilitate scoring. • No longer administered at the middle and end of first grade. • Stratification of test items to increase equivalence and consistency of scores from one form to another. • New, more explicit directions and reminders to facilitate student understanding of the task. • A checklist of common response patterns to facilitate linkages to instruction.
Nonsense Word Fluency (NWF)	• All new forms. • New and improved materials with integrated reminders to enhance the administration of the measure. • A new score, Whole Words Read (WWR), to replace Words Recoded Completely and Correctly (WRC). WWR measures the target skill of reading the words as whole words. • New font that may be more familiar to younger children. • Stratification of test items to increase equivalence and consistency of scores from one form to another. • An even distribution of vowels, with each row of five items including one word with each vowel. • New, more explicit directions and reminders facilitate student understanding of the task and clarify that the preferred responses are whole words. The student is still permitted to provide individual letter sounds or to sound out the word while learning the skills. • A checklist of common response patterns to facilitate linkages to instruction.

Table 1.3 Summary of Changes to Existing *DIBELS* Measures (continued)

Measures	Changes
***DIBELS* Oral Reading Fluency (DORF)**	• All new passages. • Passages were developed using new procedures to ensure overall equivalent difficulty with *DIBELS* (6th ed.) but with a more consistent difficulty within each grade level. • New and improved materials with integrated reminders to enhance the administration of the measure. • New font that may be more familiar to younger children in first- and second-grade passages. • New, more explicit directions and reminders to facilitate student understanding of the task. When administering three passages during benchmark assessment, shortened directions are now provided for the second and third passages. • A checklist of common response patterns to facilitate linkages to instruction.
Retell	• Retell is now included as a component of *DIBELS* Oral Reading Fluency to indicate that the end-goal of reading is to read for meaning. • New and improved materials with integrated reminders to enhance the administration of the measure. • New, more explicit directions and reminders to facilitate student understanding of the task. • A checklist of common response patterns to facilitate linkages to instruction.
Word Use Fluency–Revised (WUF-R)	• Available as an experimental measure from http://dibels.org/.

Chapter 2: **Guidelines for Administering and Scoring *DIBELS Next***

The *DIBELS* measures are standardized assessments, which means every *assessor*, or person who administers *DIBELS* to students, should administer and score the measures the same way every time with every student. A standardized assessment allows you to compare results across students or across time, or to compare student scores to a target goal. A standardized administration also ensures that the research on the reliability and validity of the measure is applicable to the obtained scores.

This chapter describes the general guidelines for administering and scoring all of the *DIBELS Next* measures. Each measure then has its own chapter with specific administration and scoring procedures for that measure. Since every measure works a bit differently, it is important to follow the correct rules for each measure.

Standard Features of *DIBELS Next* Measures

The standard features of the *DIBELS Next* measures are:

- ***Basic Early Literacy Skill:*** The core component or foundational early literacy skill that the measure assesses.
- ***Administration Time:*** The length of time for which the measure is administered, after the assessor has given directions and started the stopwatch.
- ***Administration Schedule:*** The grades and times of year in which the measure is administered for benchmark assessment.
- ***Administration Directions:*** The specific procedures to follow when administering the measure, as well as the script to say to the student.
- ***When to Start the Stopwatch:*** The point at which the stopwatch should be started for the measure.
- ***Score:*** The description of the reported score.
- ***Scoring Rules:*** Detailed marking and scoring procedures.
- ***Reminders:*** Prompts that may be given under certain circumstances. Some prompts may be given only once, others may be given as often as needed.
- ***Wait Rule:*** A rule for how long the student is allowed to hesitate on an item before the next item is presented or the student is directed to proceed.
- ***Discontinue Rule:*** A rule for discontinuing the measure if the student is unable to perform the task.

Some measures do not include every feature. All of the features are explained in detail in the chapter for each measure, and the beginning of each chapter includes a chart with a brief summary of main features.

Administration Guidelines

Equipment

Each assessor will need the following tools to administer *DIBELS* in addition to the testing materials:

- Pen or pencil
- Clipboard
- Stopwatch or timer

The timer used for *DIBELS* testing should: (a) be small enough to hold in the palm of the hand or attach to the clipboard; (b) track time accurately within one-hundredth of a second; and (c) be simple to operate. The timer may function as a stopwatch or as a countdown timer. A countdown timer should be one that makes a quiet, unobtrusive beep at the end of the countdown. A stopwatch should either be silent or make quiet, unobtrusive beeps when starting or stopping the timing.

Testing Environment

DIBELS assessment is best conducted at a small table or student desk in a relatively quiet location and at a time with minimal disruptions and noise. For example, if *DIBELS* assessment is being conducted in the classroom, it is best to use a corner of the classroom with partitions to minimize distractions, and to conduct the assessment at a time when the other students are engaged in seatwork or similar quiet activities.

The assessor should be positioned so that he/she can see the student's face and should sit near enough to the student to clearly hear what the student says. When using a desk or small table, the assessor and student might sit across from each other, and with a larger table the assessor and student might sit around the corner from each other. The assessor should hold the clipboard in such a way that the student cannot see what is being written.

Timing

It is important to time each measure according to the administration and scoring procedures for that measure. Timing allows the assessor to capture not only a student's knowledge and ability with the early literacy skills, but also the student's fluency on and confidence with the skills. A student who performs a task fluently—that is, both accurately and quickly—has learned the skill to mastery, is automatic in performing the underlying skills, and is more able to remember, maintain, and apply the skill than a student who does not. Both accuracy and fluency in early literacy skills are critical to successful reading and comprehension.

Encouragement and Reinforcement

The *DIBELS* measures are standardized assessments. What the assessor can say during testing is in bold italics in the administration procedures given in this manual. No other comments or prompts should be provided to the student as part of the testing situation. In particular, the administration scripts do not allow the assessor to tell the student if he/she is right or wrong on an item during or after the assessment; however, it is appropriate for the assessor to provide general encouragement to the student between measures (for example, between the LNF and PSF measures). It is best to reinforce the student's effort with general, non-specific statements such as, "You are working really hard."

Modeling and Practice Items

Most of the *DIBELS* measures begin with the assessor modeling the activity. Modeling is intended to clearly communicate to the student what is expected on the task, and must be presented exactly as it is stated in the administration procedures. After the model, most *DIBELS* measures then have practice items to let the student try the task, with corrective feedback to ensure he/she understands the task. The practice items and responses must be delivered exactly as they are stated in the administration procedures. The practice items and corrective feedback are intended to ensure the student understands the nature of the task and what is expected. They are not intended to teach the skill to students who have not learned the skill.

Repeating Directions or Items

If you judge that the student did not hear or understand the directions, a practice item, or a test item, you may repeat the directions or the item. If the timer is already running, the timer should continue to run while you are repeating the item. It is your responsibility as the assessor to articulate clearly and loudly enough for the student to hear. You are also responsible for ensuring that the testing environment is not too noisy or distracting, and that the student is attending adequately to the directions and items. If the student continually asks you to repeat items even when these issues have been adequately addressed, the student's hearing may need to be evaluated.

Discontinuing an Assessment

Each of the individually administered *DIBELS* measures includes a discontinue rule, as discussed previously, for students who are unable to perform the task. When following the discontinue rule, stop the measure and record a score of zero.

Invalidating an Assessment

If an error was made in administering or scoring a measure, and that error cannot be corrected without retesting the student, then the score should be discarded as invalid. Reassess the student as soon as possible using an alternate form from the progress monitoring materials.

If a student refuses to participate in the testing, do not record a score. Stop the assessment and try again on another day, perhaps with an assessor who is more familiar to the student.

If you determine that the student is not able to give his/her best performance at that time—for example, the student may not be wearing glasses or a hearing aid, seems ill or particularly nervous, or an interruption occurs such as a fire drill or an announcement—then do not test the student, or if testing has already begun, then stop the assessment. Under these circumstances, do not record a score. Reassess the student at another time using an alternate form from the progress monitoring materials.

General Scoring Guidelines

Articulation and Dialect Differences

For all *DIBELS* measures, students are never penalized for articulation or dialect differences that are part of their typical speech. For example, a student who typically says /th/ for /s/ would not be penalized on FSF for saying that the first sound in the word *see* is /th/. It is helpful for assessors to be familiar with the speech patterns of the students they assess. If a student has articulation or dialect differences that are difficult to understand, consider someone retesting the student who is more familiar with the student's articulation or dialect.

Use of the Schwa Sound

The schwa sound is the /u/ sound added to some consonant sounds. In particular, the voiced consonant sounds such as /b/, /d/, and /g/ are difficult to produce without adding a schwa, i.e., "buh" for /b/. Although teachers are encouraged to model pure production of sounds in their instruction, there is no penalty for students using the schwa sound when producing isolated consonant sounds during *DIBELS* assessment.

General *DIBELS* Reminders

Each measure includes specific reminder prompts. In addition to those reminders, there are two general reminders that apply to all individually administered measures that include written material (Letter Naming Fluency, Nonsense Word Fluency, and *DIBELS* Oral Reading Fluency):

- If the student stops and it is not a hesitation on a specific item, say ***Keep going***.
  This reminder may be used as often as needed.
- If the student loses his/her place, point. *This reminder may be used as often as needed.*

Response Patterns

At the end of each *DIBELS* administration, it is optional but often valuable to note student response patterns in the scoring booklet. Making a note of any noticeable or recurring student response patterns provides information about how the student performed on specific items and what types of errors were made. This information may be useful for planning instruction. These notes are especially useful if the person testing the student is different from the person who will be teaching the student.

Recording and Scoring Responses

DIBELS measures are designed to be recorded and scored in real time as the student is responding. At times it will be necessary to make a quick judgment about a student's response. It is important to use your best professional judgment and move on. Audiotaping is not recommended. The amount of time required to listen to and score tapes afterward makes the assessment inefficient. Additionally, it is often more difficult to score from audiotapes than scoring live due to poor sound quality and background noise.

DIBELS measures are designed so that most students will not complete a measure within the time limit. For those few students who do, simply record the score achieved. Do not prorate the scores.

The individual chapters for each measure describe how to mark and score the student responses for that measure. The following rules apply to most *DIBELS* measures:

- An underline denotes a correct response. This rule applies to Phoneme Segmentation Fluency and Nonsense Word Fluency.
- A slash mark denotes an incorrect response.
- When there is both a slash and an underline, the slash overrides the underline and the response is counted as incorrect.
- An "sc" written above a slashed response denotes a self-correction, and the response is counted as correct. The only exception is the Whole Words Read (WWR) score from Nonsense Word Fluency. The student receives a point for WWR only if his/her first response for that word is correct and complete. For more information, see Chapter 8: Nonsense Word Fluency.
- When a student provides multiple responses for the same item on Letter Naming Fluency, *DIBELS* Oral Reading Fluency, or Correct Letter Sounds (CLS) from Nonsense Word Fluency, the responses are treated as self-corrections and the student's final response is scored.

Testing Materials

DIBELS materials are available for benchmark assessment and progress monitoring for students in kindergarten through sixth grade.

Benchmark Assessment Materials

Benchmark assessment materials are organized by grade, with one set for each grade from kindergarten through sixth grade. The materials are available in grade-level Classroom Sets from Sopris (http://www.soprislearning.com/DIBELS/). The benchmark assessment materials include:

- ***Benchmark Assessment Scoring Booklet.*** A Benchmark Assessment Scoring Booklet contains all the scoring forms necessary for conducting benchmark assessment at the beginning, middle, and end of the school year for that grade, except for Daze worksheets, which are included in a separate booklet. It also includes a cover sheet on which the scores are recorded for all benchmark measures, including Daze. Each student will need one Benchmark Assessment Scoring Booklet for the year.
- ***Benchmark Assessment Book: Assessor Directions and Student Materials.*** A Benchmark Assessment Book is a flip-book that contains the student materials on one side and the assessor's directions on the other side. The student materials are those that the student needs to look at during testing. A grade-level Benchmark Assessment Book includes all of the student materials and assessor directions for administering benchmark assessments at the beginning, middle, and end of the school year for that grade, except for Daze.
- ***Daze Benchmark Assessment Student Booklet.*** Each Daze Student Booklet contains three benchmark assessment worksheets for one student, with one worksheet to be administered during each benchmark assessment, at the beginning, middle, and end of the school year. Daze benchmark assessments can be administered individually or to an entire class at once. Each student in third through sixth grade will need a Daze Benchmark Assessment Student Booklet for the year.

- ***Daze Benchmark Assessment Administration Directions and Scoring Keys.*** Daze is not included in the Assessment Book or Scoring Booklets because it can be administered to a group of students at once, so a separate book is provided that includes the administration directions and the scoring keys. The scoring keys are used to score the Daze worksheets after collecting those worksheets from the students.

Progress Monitoring Assessment Materials

Progress monitoring materials contain alternate forms, of equivalent difficulty, of the same measures administered during benchmark assessment. Not all students will need progress monitoring. Progress monitoring materials are organized by measure, since students who need progress monitoring will typically be monitored on specific measures related to the instruction they are receiving, rather than on every measure for that grade. The progress monitoring materials include the following:

- ***Progress Monitoring Scoring Booklet.*** A Progress Monitoring Scoring Booklet contains the scoring forms for 20 alternate forms of a specific measure. A booklet of 20 forms is available for FSF, PSF, NWF, and each grade level for DORF. Since some students may be monitored on out-of-grade materials, the DORF booklets specify "Levels" rather than grades. A Progress Monitoring Scoring Booklet also includes a cover sheet on which the scores are recorded and graphed.
- ***Progress Monitoring Assessment Book: Assessor Directions and Student Materials.*** A Progress Monitoring Assessment Book is a flip-book that contains the student materials on one side and the assessor's directions on the other side. The student materials are the materials that the student needs to look at during testing. There are three Progress Monitoring Assessment Books. Book A includes FSF, PSF, and NWF. Book B includes PSF, NWF, and DORF Levels 1 through 3. Book C includes DORF Levels 3 through 6. There is some overlap between the books because some students are monitored on out-of-grade materials.
- ***Daze Progress Monitoring Student Booklet.*** A Daze Student Booklet contains ten Daze worksheets for use with students in the third through sixth grade who will receive progress monitoring on Daze. Since some students may be monitored on out-of-grade materials, the Daze booklets specify "Levels" rather than grades. Daze progress monitoring assessments can be administered individually or to a group of students. A Daze Progress Monitoring Student Booklet also includes a cover sheet on which the scores are recorded and graphed. Additional alternate-form Daze worksheets for each grade are available from http://dibels.org/.
- ***Daze Progress Monitoring Administration Directions and Scoring Keys.*** Daze is not included in an Assessment Book or Scoring Booklets because it can be administered to a group of students at once. A separate book is provided that includes the Daze administration directions and the scoring keys. The scoring keys are used to score the Daze worksheets after collecting those worksheets from the students. One book is provided for each Level, 3 through 6.

Accommodations

Assessment accommodations are used for those students for whom the standard administration conditions would not produce accurate results.

Approved Accommodations for *DIBELS Next*

Approved accommodations are those accommodations that are unlikely to change how the assessment functions. When approved accommodations are used, the scores can be reported and interpreted as official *DIBELS* scores (see *Table 2.1*). Approved accommodations should be used only for students for whom the accommodations are necessary to provide an accurate assessment of student skills.

Table 2.1 Accommodations Approved for Use With *DIBELS Next*

Approved Accommodations	Appropriate Measures
The use of student materials that have been enlarged or with larger print for students with visual impairments.	LNF, NWF, DORF, Daze
The use of colored overlays, filters, or lighting adjustments for students with visual impairments.	LNF, NWF, DORF, Daze
The use of assistive technology, such as hearing aids and assistive listening devices (ALDs), for students with hearing impairments.	All
The use of a marker or ruler to focus student attention on the materials for students who are not able to demonstrate their skills adequately without one. It is good practice to attempt the assessment first without a marker or ruler and then retest with an alternate form of the assessment using a marker or ruler if needed.	LNF, NWF, DORF, Daze

Unapproved Accommodations for *DIBELS Next*

Unapproved accommodations are accommodations that are likely to change how the assessment functions. Scores from measures administered with unapproved accommodations ***should not*** be treated or reported as official *DIBELS* scores, and cannot be compared to other *DIBELS* scores or benchmark goals.

An unapproved accommodation may be used when: (a) a student cannot be tested accurately using the standardized rules or approved accommodations, but the school would still like to measure progress for that student; or (b) a student's Individualized Education Plan (IEP) requires testing with an unapproved accommodation. Scores for a student using an unapproved accommodation can be used to measure individual growth for that student.

Examples of Unapproved Accommodations

- A student with limited English proficiency may be given the directions in his/her primary language.
- A student whose IEP requires assessments to be given untimed may be administered the *DIBELS* measures without the timing component. This would measure only accuracy, not fluency.

DIBELS in Braille

A special type of accommodation for students with visual impairments is to administer *DIBELS* in braille. When using a *DIBELS* measure with braille materials, the measurement of the skill being assessed would be affected by the student's fluency with braille as well as the differences between printed text and braille text. Scores for a student being tested with *DIBELS* in braille can be used to measure individual growth for that student, and can be compared to other students who are also being tested with braille *DIBELS* materials, but should not be reported as scores that are directly comparable to the print version of *DIBELS*. For information about *DIBELS Next* in braille, visit http://dibels.org/.

Training

DIBELS was designed to be administered by educational professionals and other school-approved personnel, provided they have received sufficient training on *DIBELS* administration and scoring rules. Educational professionals and school personnel who will be interpreting *DIBELS* test results or using those results to make group- or student-level decisions should receive training in how to interpret that data.

It is the responsibility of the school-based administrator or other appropriate school leader to ensure that ample time is available for assessors to be trained prior to administering *DIBELS*, and the responsibility of each assessor to ensure that he/she is adequately trained and can administer and score *DIBELS* reliably, according to the standardized procedures.

A variety of training opportunities exist, provided by the authors of *DIBELS* at Dynamic Measurement Group (http://dibels.org/) and by Sopris (http://www.soprislearning.com/DIBELS/), the publisher of *DIBELS*.

Training on *DIBELS* should cover the following topics:

- Research on learning to read and the basic early literacy skills
- Foundations of *DIBELS*, including the purposes, design, and uses
- Administration and scoring of each measure
- Framework and procedures for data-based decision-making

Practice opportunities should take place during and after the training. Scores from practice administrations should not be used to make decisions about students. When practicing with students, use materials that those students will not receive during actual test administration.

In order to use scores for educational decisions, the assessor must reliably administer the measures according to the rules given in this manual. *Appendix 3*, pages 125–132, includes an Assessment Accuracy Checklist for each measure.

Appropriate Test Use of *DIBELS*

The *DIBELS* measures were designed for *formative assessment*, or assessment that is used to adapt teaching to meet student needs (see *Table 2.2*). Unlike high-stakes testing, which is used for decisions that have substantial consequences for students, such as retention or placement in special education, formative assessment is considered low-stakes testing because the results are used for making modifications to instruction to enhance student learning (Kaminski & Cummings, 2007).

Table 2.2 Uses of *DIBELS*

	Appropriate Uses	Inappropriate Uses
Student Level	• Identify students who may be at risk for reading difficulties • Help identify areas to target instructional support • Monitor at-risk students while they receive additional, targeted instruction	• Label, track, or grade students • Make decisions regarding retention and promotion
Systems Level	• Examine the effectiveness of a school's system of instructional supports	• Evaluate teachers • Make decisions about funding • Make decisions about rewards for improved performance or sanctions for low performance

Test Security

Test items or copies of the *DIBELS* assessments should never be used for student instruction or practice in the classroom or at home. Such practices compromise the validity and value of *DIBELS* as measurement tools. Having students practice the tests may result in artificially high scores, which could prevent those students from receiving the instruction they need.

For further information on the appropriate use of *DIBELS*, please see the position papers from the *DIBELS* authors on Dynamic Measurement Group's Web site (http://dibels.org/).

Chapter 3: **Interpreting *DIBELS Next* Data**

There are four frames of reference in providing meaning for *DIBELS* scores: (a) criterion-referenced benchmark goals and cut points for risk; (b) individually referenced interpretations; (c) local norm-referenced interpretations; and (d) systemwide norm-referenced interpretations. While all frames of reference provide valuable information about a student, the authors of *DIBELS* generally regard the criterion-referenced information as most important, followed by the individually referenced information, and then the local norm-referenced information.

These four frames of reference can be used to interpret results on individual scores and on the *DIBELS* Composite Score. The *DIBELS* Composite Score is a combination of multiple *DIBELS* scores and provides the best overall estimate of the student's reading proficiency. For more information about the *DIBELS* Composite Score as well as worksheets to calculate it, see *Appendix 6*, pages 147–154.

Criterion-Referenced Interpretations: Understanding Benchmark Goals and Cut Points for Risk

DIBELS benchmark goals are empirically derived, criterion-referenced target scores that represent adequate reading progress. A benchmark goal indicates a level of skill at which the student is likely to achieve the next *DIBELS* benchmark goal or reading outcome. Benchmark goals for *DIBELS* are based on research that examines the predictive validity of a score on a measure at a particular point in time, compared to later *DIBELS* measures and external outcome assessments. If a student achieves a benchmark goal, then the odds are in favor of that student achieving later reading outcomes if the student receives research-based instruction from a core classroom curriculum.

The *cut points* for risk indicate a level of skill below which the student is unlikely to achieve subsequent reading goals without receiving additional, targeted instructional support. Students with scores below the cut point for risk are identified as likely to need *intensive support*. Intensive support refers to interventions that incorporate something more or something different from the core curriculum or supplemental support. Intensive support might entail:

- delivering instruction in a smaller group;
- providing more instructional time or more practice;
- presenting smaller skill steps in the instructional hierarchy;
- providing more explicit modeling and instruction; and/or
- providing greater scaffolding.

Because students needing intensive support are likely to have individual and sometimes unique needs, their progress is monitored frequently and their intervention is modified dynamically to ensure adequate progress.

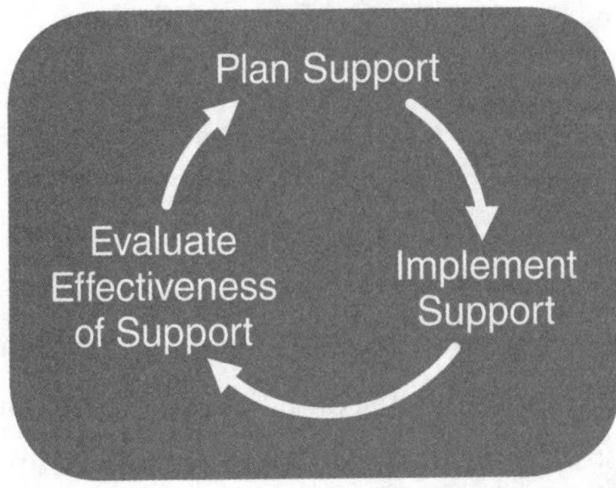

These progress monitoring steps from the Outcomes-Driven Model (see Figure 1.3, *page 8) provide an intervention feedback loop. By planning, implementing, and evaluating the effectiveness of support in an ongoing loop, the intervention can be modified dynamically to meet the student's needs.*

Students are likely to need *strategic support* when their scores are between the benchmark goal and the cut point for risk. In this range, a student's future performance is harder to predict. Strategic instructional support is carefully targeted additional support in the skill areas where the student is having difficulty. These students should be monitored regularly to ensure they are making adequate progress, and should receive increased or modified support, if necessary, to achieve subsequent reading goals.

To gain a better understanding of what *DIBELS* results mean in a local context, districts and schools can examine the linkages between the *DIBELS* benchmark goals and cut points for risk and their own outcome assessments, such as state-level criterion-referenced tests. By comparing *DIBELS* measures to an outcomes assessment (e.g., Buck & Torgesen, 2003; Wilson, 2005), and by calculating conditional probabilities (e.g., "80% of students at benchmark on *DIBELS* ORF at the end of third grade met the Proficient level on the state criterion-referenced test."), schools can determine how the *DIBELS* benchmark goals compare to their own external criteria.

A score at or above the benchmark goal indicates that the odds are in the student's favor of achieving the next goal, but it is not a guarantee. For example, if students at or above the benchmark goal have an 85% chance of meeting the next goal, that means that 15% of students in the benchmark range may not achieve that goal. Some students who achieve scores at or above the benchmark goal may still need supplemental support to achieve the next goal. It is important to attend to other indicators of risk when planning support for students, such as attendance, behavior, motivation, vocabulary and language skills, and other related skill areas.

The *DIBELS Next* benchmark and cut points for risk can be found in *Appendix 5*, pages 137–146.

Table 3.1 provides interpretations of student performance with respect to the benchmark goals and cut points for risk.

Table 3.1 Student Performance Interpretations

Score Level	Likely need for support to achieve subsequent early literacy goals	Interpretation
At or Above Benchmark *scores at or above the benchmark goal*	Likely to Need Core Support	The odds are in the student's favor (approximately 80%–90%) of achieving subsequent early literacy goals. The student is making adequate progress in reading and is likely to achieve subsequent reading benchmarks with appropriate and effective instruction. The student needs continuing effective curriculum and instruction.
Below Benchmark *scores below the benchmark goal and at or above the cut point for risk*	Likely to Need Strategic Support	The odds of achieving subsequent early literacy goals are roughly 40%–60% for a student with skills in this range. The student typically needs strategic, targeted instructional support to ensure that he/she makes adequate progress and achieves subsequent reading benchmarks.
Well Below Benchmark *scores below the cut point for risk*	Likely to Need Intensive Support	The odds of achieving subsequent early literacy goals are approximately 10%–20% for a student whose performance is below the cut point for risk. The student is unlikely to achieve subsequent reading benchmarks unless provided with substantial, intensive instructional support.

Individually Referenced Interpretations: Analyzing Student Growth and Progress Over Time

In addition to information on where a student is performing relative to the benchmark goals and cut points for risk, *DIBELS* also allows interpretations based on where the student's skills are relative to their past performance. For example, even though a student's Oral Reading Fluency score of 45 words correct per minute might be below the cut point for risk, the score of 45 might represent substantial progress compared to previous scores. For individually referenced interpretations, *DIBELS* results are used to examine individual student performance over time. Evaluating student growth is essential in determining whether the student is making adequate progress toward later goals. Examining student growth (i.e., progress monitoring) is also essential in Response-to-Intervention (RtI) models of service delivery and educational decision-making. Progress monitoring helps the teacher decide whether the instructional support the student is receiving is adequately addressing the student's needs, or whether changes should be made to that support.

Local Norm-Referenced Interpretations: Comparing Students Districtwide

Local norms allow a school or district to compare an individual student's performance to other students in the district. Local norms have the important advantage of being representative of the student's district. Another important advantage is that local norms can be updated yearly. If a district's population changes over time, local norms from the current year will continue to be representative of that population. Although local norms are representative of the district, they are not necessarily representative of the national population. If the average achievement in a given school is below the national average achievement score, all percentile ranks would be affected. For example, the score at the 40th percentile in a low-performing district may be at the 20th percentile in a high-performing district. Local normative comparisons also can be problematic when a small number of students are included. All students in the district should be included when determining local norms, but small districts may not have enough students for stable local normative comparisons. Most data management services for *DIBELS* data will provide local norms.

Local norms can be valuable for a district when making decisions about providing additional support for students. Districts have the flexibility of choosing a level, based on local norms, below which students are provided with additional instructional support. Districts can make this choice based on any pertinent considerations, including financial and staff resources. If a district is able to provide support to 50% of students, students may be selected for support who are at the 50th percentile or lower on *DIBELS*. If a district is able to provide additional support to only 15% of students, students can be selected who are at the 15th percentile or lower on *DIBELS*. By using district-wide local norms, students with equivalent needs in different schools can be provided with support.

For norm-referenced interpretations with *DIBELS*, descriptors for levels of performance are provided in *Table 3.2*. The performance descriptors are intended to describe the current level of skill for the student in comparison to other students in the district. They are not intended as statements about what the student is capable of learning with appropriate effective instruction.

Table 3.2 Levels of Performance

Percentile Ranges	**Performance Descriptors** *Compared to other students in the school or district, the student's performance is:*
98th percentile and above	Upper Extreme
91st to 97th percentile	Well-Above Average
76th to 90th percentile	Above Average
25th to 75th percentile	Average
9th to 24th percentile	Below Average
3rd to 8th percentile	Well-Below Average
2nd percentile and below	Lower Extreme

Systemwide or National Norm-Referenced Interpretations: Comparing Students in a Larger Context

Once *DIBELS Next* has been implemented for a year, systemwide normative comparisons are likely to be available from the major data management services that support *DIBELS*. Systemwide norms allow a school or district to compare a student's performance to other students in that system. A disadvantage of systemwide norms is that they may not be representative of the characteristics of students in a particular district. For example, a local district may have a very high proportion of English language learners. While the systemwide norms may include English language learners, the proportion may or may not be representative of the local district. A second disadvantage of systemwide norms is that they may or may not be representative of the national distribution of characteristics. A very broad data management service may be more representative, while a data management service for a particular state may be less representative of the nation, but more representative of the state. It is important for district and school leaders to obtain information about the norm sample and assess its relevance to their particular demographic prior to making decisions about students or overall district performance.

The primary value of national or systemwide normative information is to provide an alternative perspective on student performance. When the system-wide norms are based on a large and nationally representative sample of students, they can provide an indication of national student achievement in early reading. For instance, if 120 words correct on DORF at the end of third grade is at the 50th percentile in local district norms, and is at the 60th percentile on systemwide norms, then the average achievement in the district is above the national average. Similarly, at an individual student level, a student might be at the 55th percentile compared to local norms, but might be at the 5th percentile compared to systemwide norms. In this context, the student might appear to be making adequate progress but the systemwide normative information clarifies that the student is still of concern in a larger context. Considering local norms and systemwide norms can provide a balanced perspective on the student's skills and needs.

The Importance of Response Patterns

In addition to interpreting scores from a criterion-referenced, individually referenced, local norm-referenced, or systemwide norm-referenced perspective, the pattern of behavior that the student displays on the assessment is also important (see *Figure 3.1*). *DIBELS* measures are designed to be indicators of basic early literacy skills. If the student achieves a score above the benchmark goal but does so in a way that indicates that the early literacy skill has not been mastered, the student may still need additional support to be on track. For example, if a student reaches the benchmark goal on Phoneme Segmentation Fluency but does so by rapidly segmenting words in an onset-rime pattern (/m/ /ap/, /str/ /eat/), that student may not be as likely to reach the next goal as a student who achieves the benchmark goal by correctly segmenting phonemes (/m/ /a/ /p/, /s/ /t/ /r/ /ea/ /t/). (See *Appendix 1*, page 115, for a pronunciation guide that shows how individual phonemes are represented on PSF.) For this reason, each measure includes a checklist of common, instructionally relevant response patterns. Teachers and other specialists who interpret *DIBELS* results to provide instruction for students should review the types of responses for students in their classes. This information, in addition to the raw scores, can dramatically guide instructional strategies.

Figure 3.1 **Phoneme Segmentation Fluency Response Patterns**

PSF Response Patterns
☐ Repeats word
☐ Makes random errors
☐ Says initial sound only
☒ Says onset rime
☐ Does not segment blends
☐ Adds sounds
☐ Makes consistent errors on specific sound(s)
☐ Other

An example of PSF response patterns for a student who responds with an onset-rime pattern rather than correctly segmenting phonemes.

Chapter 4: **Implementing *DIBELS Next* in Your School**

DIBELS assessment is conducted in two ways: benchmark assessment and progress monitoring. Benchmark assessment is the process of universally screening all students in a grade, school, or district three times per year. There are two primary purposes for conducting benchmark assessment: (a) identifying students who may not be on track to reach important reading outcomes; and (b) providing schoolwide indices of status and progress. Students who are identified as not being on track during benchmark assessment are likely to need additional instructional assistance to reach future benchmark goals. Progress monitoring is the more frequent, ongoing measurement of individual student growth for students who are receiving additional instructional assistance, to ensure that those students are making adequate progress.

Conducting Benchmark Assessment

When to Test

Benchmark assessment is conducted three times per school year, at the beginning, middle, and end of the year. Recommended testing windows are shown in *Table 4.1*.

Table 4.1 Benchmark Assessment Yearly Schedule

Time of Year	Beginning of Year Benchmark 1	Middle of Year Benchmark 2	End of Year Benchmark 3
Recommended testing windows	Months 1 to 3 of the school year	Months 4 to 6 of the school year	Months 7 to 9 of the school year
Most frequent benchmark month	Month 1	Month 5	Month 9
Example benchmark schedule for a district with a September to June school calendar	September	January	May

Benchmark assessment can take place any time within the recommended testing windows. However, the times provided as examples are most closely aligned with the timing of the *DIBELS* benchmark goals.

When a school district schedules the time within that window when testing will actually take place, all testing should occur within a two- to three-week timeframe so that students have had roughly the same amount of instructional time. When scheduling benchmark assessments, it may be helpful to use the school calendar to avoid other assessments, holidays, and important school events. There should be a roughly equal amount of time between benchmark assessments, and one to two weeks after the start of school or a major break should be allowed to give students time to adjust.

Who Administers Benchmark Assessment

Any educator who has been trained on *DIBELS* administration and scoring can conduct *DIBELS* benchmark assessments. This might include classroom teachers, special educators, reading specialists, instructional assistants, principals, related service personnel such as speech/language therapists and school psychologists, counselors, central office administrators, and librarians. It is important that the data are shared with those who teach the student, regardless of who administers the testing.

Testing Approaches

Multiple approaches to conducting *DIBELS* benchmark assessment are possible. Each approach has advantages and disadvantages. Selecting an approach will depend on the resources and characteristics of a particular school or district. Three common approaches are detailed below.

Within Classroom. The within-classroom approach involves classroom teachers, and their assistants when available, conducting benchmark assessment on all of their students. Typically this approach consists of using a portion of class time each day over the designated testing window to assess students. For example, in a classroom with 25 students, the assessment could be completed in one week by assessing 5 students per day. An advantage of this approach is that classroom teachers can participate in assessing all of their students. A disadvantage is that this approach takes time away from instruction. In addition, it may promote a within-classroom as opposed to a schoolwide approach to providing support to change literacy outcomes.

Schoolwide: One Day. The schoolwide approach to conducting benchmark assessment in one day involves a large team of trained assessors. In this approach, the team assesses a class at a time, typically completing an entire class within 30 minutes. If classroom teachers participate in testing their own students, a substitute teacher or assistant may cover the classroom during that block of time. Assessors may be stationed in a central location, such as the library, or may be stationed around the school in designated assessment locations. To complete the benchmark assessment in one day, the team needs to be large enough to cycle through the school. Advantages of this approach include efficient testing and minimal disruption to instruction in each classroom. Disadvantages include the need for a large team of trained assessors, the potential for disruption to special services for the day if support staff are involved, and, if needed, funding for substitute teachers and/or additional assessors.

Schoolwide: Multiple Days. The multi-day schoolwide approach uses a smaller team to cycle through all of the classrooms in a school. An advantage of this approach is that it requires a smaller assessment team. A disadvantage is that it takes longer overall to collect the benchmark data.

Time Required for Testing

The amount of time it will take to complete the benchmark assessment for each student will vary by grade and time of year. *Table 4.2* provides an estimate of the time required per student.

Table 4.2 Estimated Time Requirements for Benchmark Assessments

	Beginning of Year		Middle of Year		End of Year	
	Measures	Time	Measures	Time	Measures	Time
Kindergarten	FSF, LNF	3 minutes	FSF, PSF, LNF, NWF	6.5 minutes	LNF, PSF, NWF	5 minutes
First	LNF, PSF, NWF	5 minutes	NWF, DORF	8 minutes	NWF, DORF	8 minutes
Second	NWF, DORF	8 minutes	DORF	6 minutes	DORF	6 minutes
Third to Sixth	DORF	6 minutes per student	DORF	6 minutes per student	DORF	6 minutes per student
	Daze	5 minutes for group testing, 1–2 minutes scoring time per worksheet	Daze	5 minutes for group testing, 1–2 minutes scoring time per worksheet	Daze	5 minutes for group testing, 1–2 minutes scoring time per worksheet

Managing Materials

The benchmark assessment will go more smoothly if the materials are prepared ahead of time. It may be helpful to assign one person in the district and at each school to manage the materials. In addition to the assessment materials listed in *Chapter 2*, pages 19 and 20, each assessor will need a pen or pencil, stopwatch or timer, and a clipboard.

It is helpful to have the scoring booklets prepared ahead of time. Labels can be printed with the student name and ID number, teacher name, school, and school year ahead of time and attached to the scoring booklets. Then the booklets can be grouped by classroom for efficient use on the day of assessment.

Ensuring Accurate Results

In order to interpret the results of testing and use that data to make decisions about instruction, it is important that the measures are administered and scored correctly. To ensure the accuracy of the data, the following steps can be taken:

- All assessors must be trained as detailed in *Chapter 2*, page 22, and should practice until they can reliably administer the measures according to the rules given in this manual. *Appendix 3*, pages 125–132, includes Assessment Accuracy Checklists that can be used during practice to check the assessor's accuracy.
- The administration and scoring procedures detailed in this manual should be reviewed before each benchmark period, with periodic accuracy checks for all assessors.
- Shadow-scoring is one way to be sure that each assessor is giving and scoring *DIBELS* according to the standardized procedures. Shadow-scoring involves two assessors working

with a student at the same time. One assessor interacts with the student and administers the measures while the other is simultaneously timing and scoring, using the Assessment Accuracy Checklists to provide constructive feedback. At the end of the assessment, the two assessors compare timing and scores. A general guideline is that both assessors should be within 2 points of each other on each score. This manual serves as a reference to resolve any disagreement.

- To ensure that the scores used for decision-making are the scores that students actually received, check that the scores were calculated correctly and entered into the data management system correctly. It is recommended that approximately 10% of student booklets be rescored to check for accuracy, and that 10% of the scores on the booklets are checked against the scores entered in the system.

Establishing Rapport

An assessor who is unfamiliar to the student being tested may engage the student in a brief conversation prior to the assessment. This helps put the student at ease and provides a brief sample of language to identify articulation errors. The assessor should also make eye contact with the student during the assessment. Although the directions must be read verbatim, they should be read in a friendly tone of voice, and not a monotone. The priority is to follow standard procedures while still getting the best possible performance from the child. Be sensitive to any needs or issues that may come up for the student during the assessment.

Measures Used in Benchmark Assessment

Benchmark assessment includes a number of different measures based on the grade and time of year, and is always administered using grade-level materials. The measures to administer are identified on the cover page of the benchmark scoring booklet (see *Figures 4.1* and *4.2* on pages 35 and 36). For all measures except Daze, scoring forms are included in the scoring booklet, and student materials are included in the benchmark assessment book for that grade. For Daze, students fill out separate worksheets. The benchmark time periods are identified by a number and a label. Benchmark 1 is used at the beginning of the school year, and is identified as Beginning; Benchmark 2 is used in the middle of the school year, and is identified as Middle; and Benchmark 3 is used at the end of the school year, and is identified as End. Note that for *DIBELS* Oral Reading Fluency, three passages are administered for each benchmark assessment, and the median (middle) score is recorded. Using the median score from three passages gives the best indicator of student performance over a range of different text and content.

In most cases, the *DIBELS* benchmark measures that are individually administered should be given to a student in a single sitting in the order in which they appear in the scoring booklet. If a student has difficulty focusing for the amount of time necessary to complete all measures, it may be necessary to assess the student in multiple sessions. Daze can be administered to an entire class at once, and can be given before or after the students have been tested on the other measures.

Data Management and Reporting

After the benchmark testing is complete, the data should be organized so that educators can access and use the results easily. It is useful to collect benchmark data only if they are then used for planning instruction. The first step is to record the scores on the cover page of the scoring booklet for easy access. *Figure 4.1* and

Figure 4.1 Example of a First Grade Benchmark Scoring Booklet Cover Sheet

GRADE 1

DIBELS Next

Benchmark Assessment

First Grade Scoring Booklet

Name: Samantha

Student ID: 447523 School Year: 2010-2011

Teacher: Smith

School: Glenoaks Elementary

		1 Beginning			2 Middle			3 End		
Date		9/14/09			1/21/10			5/15/10		
LNF		54								
PSF		33								
NWF	CLS	24			48			65		
	WWR	0			7			13		
DORF (Circle the median score)	Passage				1	2	3	1	2	3
	Words Correct				(13)	15	12	(42)	40	64
	Errors				(10)	8	11	6	4	(5)
	Accuracy				57%			89%		
	Retell							20	(32)	47
	Retell Quality							2	(2)	3

Revised 04/06/10

Cambium Learning Group | Sopris

Figure 4.2 Example of a Fourth Grade Benchmark Scoring Booklet Cover Sheet

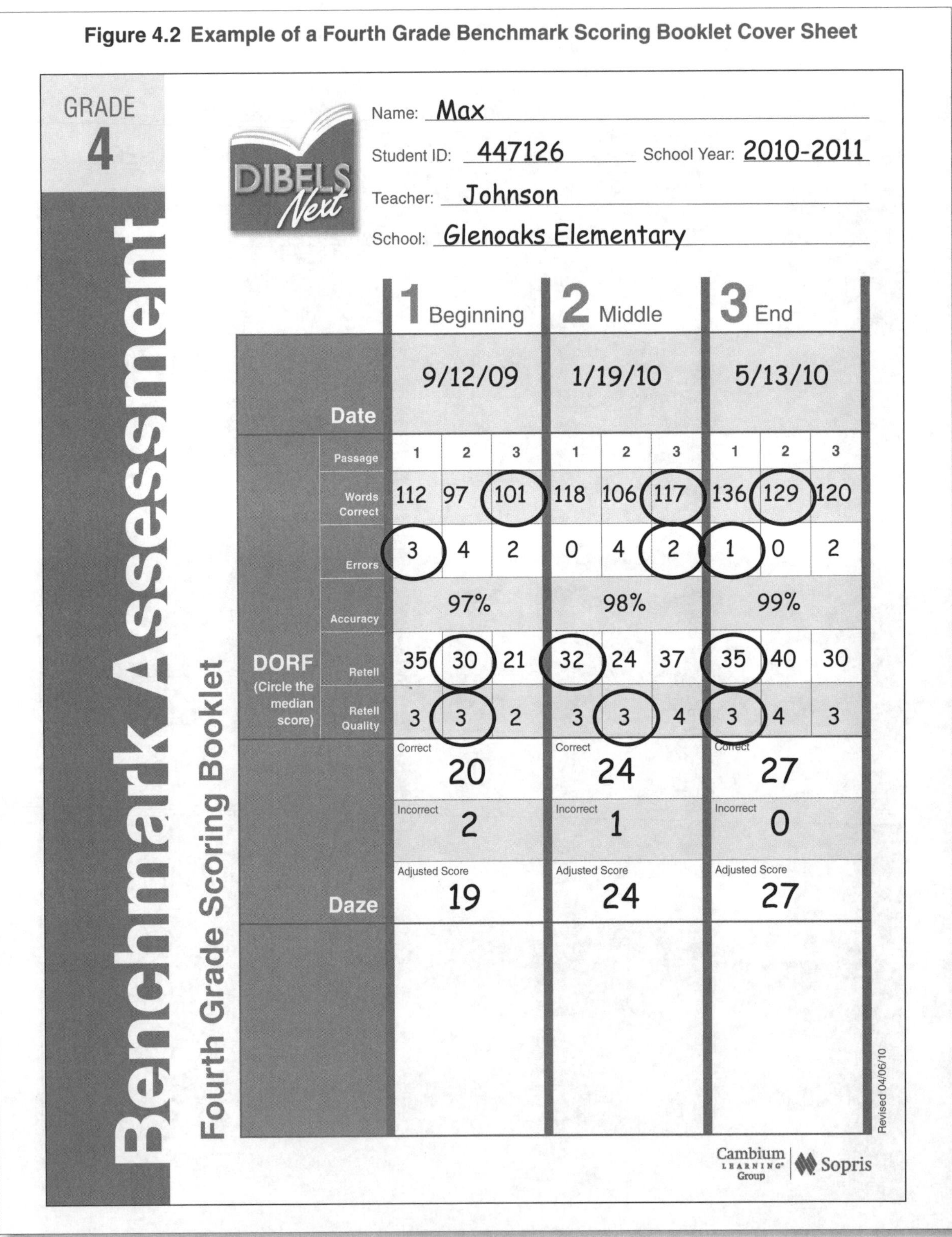

GRADE 4

Benchmark Assessment

Fourth Grade Scoring Booklet

DIBELS Next

Name: Max

Student ID: 447126 School Year: 2010-2011

Teacher: Johnson

School: Glenoaks Elementary

		1 Beginning			2 Middle			3 End		
Date		9/12/09			1/19/10			5/13/10		
DORF (Circle the median score)	Passage	1	2	3	1	2	3	1	2	3
	Words Correct	112	97	101	118	106	117	136	129	120
	Errors	3	4	2	0	4	2	1	0	2
	Accuracy	97%			98%			99%		
	Retell	35	30	21	32	24	37	35	40	30
	Retell Quality	3	3	2	3	3	4	3	4	3
Daze	Correct	20			24			27		
	Incorrect	2			1			0		
	Adjusted Score	19			24			27		

Revised 04/06/10

Cambium Learning Group | Sopris

Figure 4.2 show examples of how to record student information and scores on the cover pages of the benchmark scoring booklets.

The next step is to record the results in a data management system that can then summarize and report the data in way that is useful for teachers and administrators. Options include organizing results in a table or spreadsheet, or using a web-based data management service that allows for entry and reporting of *DIBELS* scores. An advantage of a data management service is that, once the student scores are entered, reports are available immediately at the district, school, grade, classroom, and individual student levels. A variety of options are available for managing *DIBELS* data, but it is important to use a system that provides results quickly and presents those results in ways that help teachers and administrators make decisions about instruction.

Data management options include:

- The *DIBELS* Data System from the University of Oregon. http://dibels.uoregon.edu/
- VPORT from Sopris, the publisher of *DIBELS*. http://www.voyagerlearning.com/vport/
- mCLASS from Wireless Generation, for users of the handheld version of *DIBELS*. http://www.wirelessgeneration.com/

Conducting Progress Monitoring

Progress monitoring is done with students who are not on track with important early literacy skills at the time of the *DIBELS* benchmark assessment. The purpose of progress monitoring is to provide ongoing feedback to the teacher about the effectiveness of instruction and to make timely decisions about changes to instruction so that students will meet grade-level goals. Progress monitoring involves ongoing assessment of target skills for students who are receiving instruction in those skills.

The standardized procedures for administering a *DIBELS* measure apply when using *DIBELS* for progress monitoring.

Identifying Students for Progress Monitoring

Students who are below the benchmark goal on one or more measures may receive progress monitoring assessment in targeted areas that are the focus of instruction or intervention. Teachers may also choose to monitor any other students about whose progress they have concerns. For example, if a student has met the benchmark goal but has highly variable performance, poor attendance, or behavioral issues, the teacher may choose to monitor that student, particularly if the student's score is just above the benchmark goal.

Selecting *DIBELS* Measures for Progress Monitoring

Students should be monitored in material that matches the skill area or areas targeted for instruction. In most cases, progress monitoring will focus on one measure only, which should represent the student's instructional level of the skill area targeted for instruction. Sometimes it is appropriate to monitor a student using more than one *DIBELS* measure. For example, a second-grade student might be monitored once per week with NWF and once per month with first grade DORF as a way to track acquisition of the alphabetic principle and the application of those skills to connected text.

Progress monitoring forms should be administered in the order they appear in the booklet. Note that for DORF, while three passages are administered during benchmark assessment, a single passage is administered each time for progress monitoring. Educational decisions are based on at least three test administrations.

Material selected for progress monitoring must be sensitive to growth, yet still represent an ambitious goal. The appropriate monitoring level can be identified using survey-level assessment, or "testing back" until the appropriate level is found. Material that is too difficult will not be sensitive to small changes in student skill and can result in student and teacher frustration as well as inaccurate decisions about the effectiveness of instruction. Material that is too easy will not leave enough distance between the current level of student performance and the goal, likely resulting in lowered expectations and less progress. For students who are performing below grade level, the purpose of progress monitoring is to provide information to guide instruction, with the primary goal of instruction being to improve student progress and bring the student up to grade-level performance.

Data Management and Reporting

The front cover of each *DIBELS* progress monitoring scoring booklet includes a graph to record the scores. Progress monitoring data should be graphed and readily available to those who teach the student. An aimline should be drawn from the student's current skill level (which may be the most recent benchmark assessment score) to the goal. Progress monitoring scores can then be plotted over time and examined to determine whether they indicate that the student is making adequate progress (i.e., fall above or below the aimline). *Figure 4.3* is an example of how to record student information and scores on a progress monitoring scoring booklet cover sheet, as well as how to graph the scores and draw an aimline.

Figure 4.3 Example of a First Grade Progress Monitoring Scoring Booklet Cover Sheet

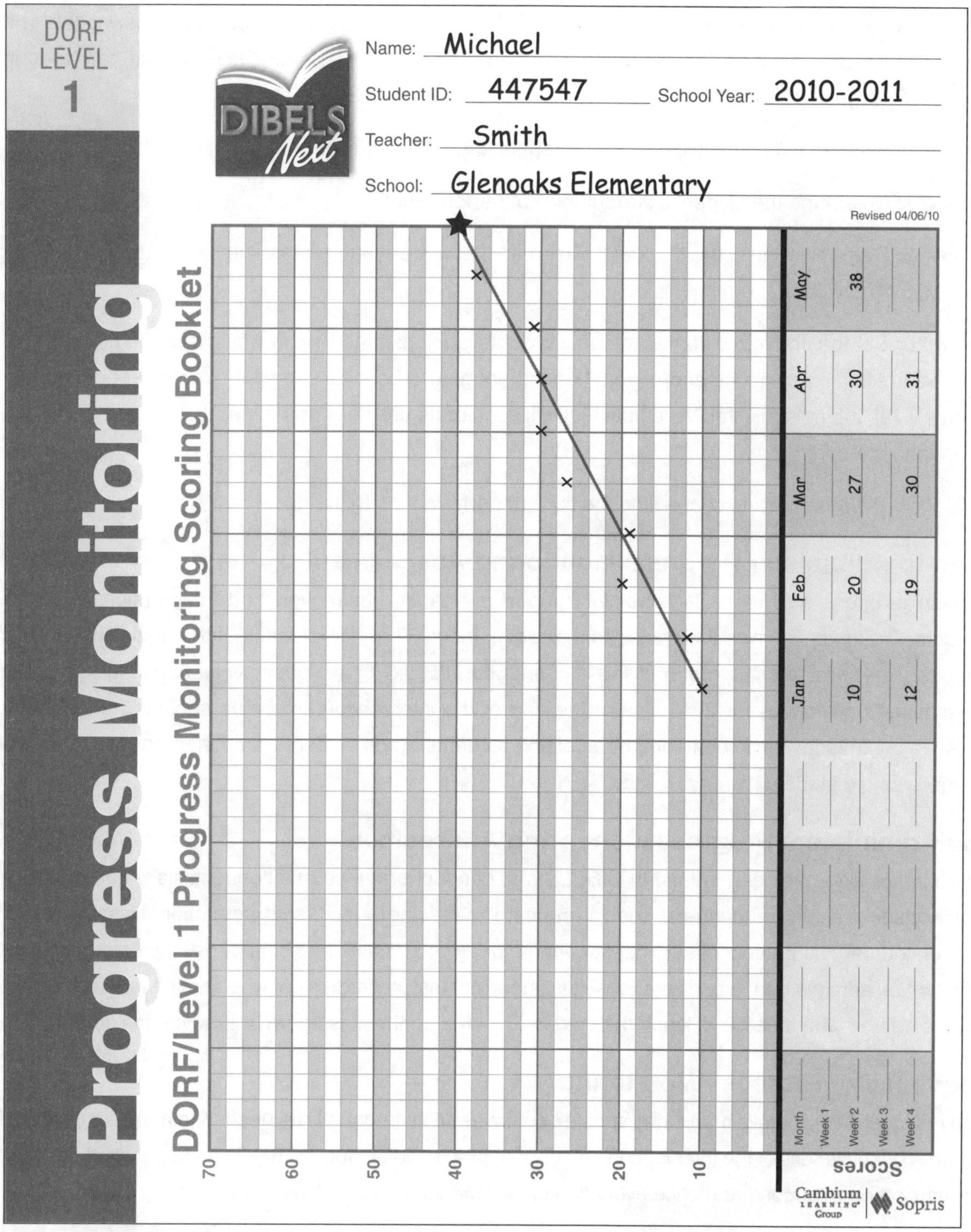

DORF LEVEL 1

DIBELS *Next*

Name: Michael

Student ID: 447547 School Year: 2010-2011

Teacher: Smith

School: Glenoaks Elementary

Revised 04/06/10

Progress Monitoring

DORF/Level 1 Progress Monitoring Scoring Booklet

70 60 50 40 30 20 10

Scores

Month	Week 1	Week 2	Week 3	Week 4
Jan		10		12
Feb		20		19
Mar		27		30
Apr		30		31
May		38		

Cambium Learning Group | Sopris

Setting Progress Monitoring Goals

A progress monitoring goal has two components: the score to aim for and the timeframe in which to reach it. When monitoring a student in grade-level materials, use the standard *DIBELS* benchmark goals and the standard timeframe in which they should be reached. Benchmark goals for *DIBELS Next* can be found in *Appendix 5*, pages 137–146.

When monitoring a student in below-grade materials, the following steps are recommended:

Step 1: Determine the student's current level of performance.

Step 2: Determine the score to aim for based on the end-of-year goal for the level of materials being used for monitoring.

Step 3: Set the timeframe so that the goal is achieved in half the time in which it would normally be achieved (e.g., moving the end-of-year benchmark goal to be achieved by the mid-year benchmark date). The intent is to establish a goal that will accelerate progress and support a student to catch up to their peers.

Step 4: Draw an aimline connecting the current performance to the goal.

When to Administer Progress Monitoring Assessment

Although progress monitoring is a helpful support to reading instruction and intervention, it should be conducted so as to minimize time taken from reading instruction. For example, if the decision is to monitor progress weekly for a small group of five students on *DIBELS* Oral Reading Fluency, one student could be assessed on Monday for 2 minutes at the end of the intervention time. The second student could be assessed on Tuesday, and so on for the remaining students. Each student would then be monitored weekly, but only a single student per day.

Who Administers Progress Monitoring Assessment

Any educator who has been trained in *DIBELS* can conduct progress monitoring. This group of educators might include classroom teachers, special educators, reading specialists, instructional assistants, principals, related service personnel such as speech/language therapists and school psychologists, counselors, central office administrators, and librarians. It is important that, regardless of who administers the testing, the data are shared with those who teach the student, whether in the classroom or intervention setting.

Frequency of Progress Monitoring

Students receiving progress monitoring should be monitored as frequently as needed to make timely decisions about the effectiveness of the intervention. In general, this would be approximately once per week for students receiving intensive support and once every two to four weeks for students receiving strategic support.

Making Decisions With Progress Monitoring Data

Progress monitoring data should be reviewed at regular intervals. This review can be done by a classroom teacher and/or a team of educators working with a student. In general, if three consecutive data points fall below the aimline, the team should meet and make a considered decision about maintaining or modifying the instruction. If the student's progress is not likely to result in meeting the goal, then instruction should be changed. The overarching goal is to make good decisions regarding instruction to improve student outcomes.

Communicating With Students, Parents, and School Personnel

Preparing Students for *DIBELS* Benchmark Assessment

Before each of the three benchmark assessments, teachers may make a statement to the class about the testing and about what students can expect to experience. The goal of the statement is to inform students and put them at ease, while encouraging them to do their best. It may be helpful to introduce the adults who will participate in the assessment and announce the locations where it will take place. A Sample Student Statement is included in *Appendix 4*, page 133.

Informing Parents About *DIBELS* Assessment

Parents and guardians are important partners in improving reading outcomes. It is good policy to communicate to parents about the assessment tools used at school. Information to communicate might include:

- an explanation of the skills that are measured by *DIBELS* and why those skills are important;
- who will see the results;
- how and when parents will receive information about their child's performance;
- how the results will be used; and
- who to contact for more information.

A Sample Parent Announcement Letter and a Sample Results Letter are included in *Appendix 4*, pages 134–136.

Sharing Results With Parents

Following each benchmark assessment, *DIBELS* results may be communicated to each student's parents or guardians. The communication might include what the expectation for adequate progress is for that grade and time of year, how the student performed relative to that expectation, and any appropriate next steps. A Sample Results Letter is included in *Appendix 4*, pages 135 and 136. *DIBELS* results also may be shared and discussed at parent-teacher conferences.

DIBELS progress monitoring information may also be communicated to parents or guardians. When progress monitoring occurs in the context of general education support, the procedures may be discussed with parents, including the educational concerns, the instructional support that is being provided, who will be collecting progress monitoring data, and how often the data will be shared. Engaging parents as partners in working toward important literacy goals can be a powerful strategy for improving student outcomes. When progress monitoring is part of an evaluation for special education eligibility, appropriate informed consent procedures should be followed.

Sharing Results With School Personnel

Following each benchmark assessment, schedule time to discuss and analyze the *DIBELS* data with classroom teachers and other appropriate support staff who teach those students. An efficient way to review the results is during a grade-level meeting that includes resource staff who support that grade. In addition to reviewing the results in a meeting, the data should be made readily accessible to the classroom teachers and support staff who need to use it for making ongoing decisions about instruction.

Basic Early Literacy Skill	*DIBELS* Indicator
Phonemic Awareness	First Sound Fluency

What is phonemic awareness?

Phonemic awareness is the explicit awareness that spoken words are made up of individual sounds or phonemes. A phoneme is the smallest sound unit into which speech can be divided that makes a difference to the meaning of the word (National Reading Panel, 2000). Phonemic awareness involves the ability to attend to and manipulate these phonemes in spoken words. For example, the knowledge that the word *dog* begins with the sound /d/ is phonemic awareness. The ability to replace the /d/ sound at the beginning of *dog* with the /h/ sound to make the word *hog* is also phonemic awareness. Phonemic awareness is an auditory skill that does not require knowledge of the letters of the alphabet or letter-sound knowledge, thus it is not the same as phonics.

A convergence of research on the acquisition of reading skills has demonstrated that phonemic awareness is highly predictive of success in learning to read (Gillon, 2004; Stahl & Murray, 2006). Additionally, effective instruction in phonemic awareness leads to significant differences in reading achievement (Ehri, 2004; National Reading Panel, 2000). Most reading researchers advocate that phonemic awareness be purposefully and explicitly taught as part of a comprehensive instructional program in reading and writing.

Chapter 5: *DIBELS* First Sound Fluency (FSF)

Overview

Basic Early Literacy Skill	Phonemic Awareness
Administration Time	1 minute
Administration Schedule	Beginning of kindergarten to middle of kindergarten
Score	2 points for each correct initial phoneme and 1 point for each correct initial consonant blend, consonant plus vowel, or consonant blend plus vowel said by the student in 1 minute
Wait Rule	If the student does not respond within 3 seconds on a word, mark a slash (/) through the zero and say the next word.
Discontinue Rule	Zero points in the first five words

What is FSF?

First Sound Fluency (FSF) is a new measure in *DIBELS Next*. FSF is a brief, direct measure of a student's fluency in identifying the initial sounds in words. The ability to isolate the first sound in a word is an important phonemic awareness skill that is highly related to reading acquisition and reading achievement (Yopp, 1988). The ability to isolate and identify the first phoneme in a word is an easier skill than segmenting words or manipulating phonemes in words, thus FSF is used as a measure of developing phonemic awareness at the beginning and middle of kindergarten.

Using standardized directions, the assessor says a series of words one at a time to the student and asks the student to say the first sound in the word. On the scoring page, the assessor circles the corresponding sound or group of sounds the student says. *Appendix 1*, page 115, provides a pronunciation guide for how individual sounds are represented on the FSF measure. Students receive either 2 points for saying the initial phoneme of a word (e.g., /s/ in *sit*) or 1 point for saying the initial consonant blend (e.g., /st/, /str/ in *street*), consonant plus vowel (e.g., /si/ in *sit*), or consonant blend plus vowel (e.g., /strea/ in *street*). A response is scored as correct as long as the student provides any of the correct responses listed for the word. The total score is based on the number of correct 1- and 2-point responses the student says in 1 minute.

Differential scoring for student responses allows young students to receive partial credit for demonstrating beginning skills in phonemic awareness. A student who may not be able to isolate an initial phoneme (e.g., /s/, /d/) would still receive partial credit for providing the first group of sounds in the word, showing emerging understanding that words are made up of sounds. Although partial credit is given, the goal is for the student to be able to correctly say the first phoneme of each word.

To ensure that students understand the task and to maximize the performance of young students who may not have had any prior exposure to instruction in phonemic awareness, three practice items are included. The practice items provide increasing levels of support, including modeling (e.g., "listen to me say . . .") and leading the correct response (e.g., "say it with me"). By design, the first two practice items start with the same sound, /m/. In the first practice item, isolation of the /m/ sound at the beginning of a word is modeled. In the second practice item, the student is asked to isolate the beginning sound in a word that also starts with /m/. In the third practice item, the student is asked to generalize the skill of isolating beginning sounds to a word that does not start with /m/.

Materials

- Scoring Booklet
- Assessment Book
- Pen/pencil
- Clipboard
- Stopwatch

Administration Directions

Follow these directions exactly each time with each student. Say the words in bold italic type verbatim. Begin with the modeling and practice activities. The practice activities are designed to introduce the assessment task to the student. They are untimed and include correction procedures. The correction procedures are not used once the timing begins.

▶ **Practice item #1)** ***Listen to me say this word, "man." The first sound that you hear in the word "man" is /mmm/. Listen. /mmm/. "Man." What is the first sound you hear in the word "man"?***

<table>
<tr><td>Correct response
/mmm/ or /ma/</td><td colspan="5">Good. /mmm/ is the first sound in "man."</td><td>(Present practice item #2.)</td></tr>
<tr><td rowspan="3">Incorrect response
Student does not respond within 3 <u>seconds</u> or responds <u>incorrectly</u></td><td rowspan="3">/mmm/ is the first sound you hear in the word "man." Listen. /mmm/. "Man." Say it with me. /mmm/. Let's try it again. What is the first sound you hear in the word "man"?</td><td>Correct response</td><td colspan="3">Good.</td><td>(Present practice item #2.)</td></tr>
<tr><td rowspan="2">Incorrect response</td><td rowspan="2">/mmm/. Say /mmm/.</td><td>Correct</td><td>Good.</td><td>(Present practice item #2.)</td></tr>
<tr><td>Incorrect</td><td>Okay.</td><td>(Present practice item #2.)</td></tr>
</table>

▶ **Practice item #2)** ***Listen to me say another word, "moon." What is the first sound you hear in the word "moon"?***

<table>
<tr><td>*Correct response*
/mmm/ or /moo/</td><td>***Good. /mmm/ is the first sound in "moon."***</td><td>(Present practice item #3.)</td></tr>
</table>

<table>
<tr><td rowspan="3">*Incorrect response*
Student does not respond within 3 <u>seconds</u> or responds <u>incorrectly</u></td><td rowspan="3">***/mmm/ is the first sound you hear in the word "moon." Listen. /mmm/. "Moon." Say it with me. /mmm/. Let's try it again. What is the first sound you hear in the word "moon"?***</td><td>*Correct response*</td><td>**Good.**</td><td colspan="3">(Present practice item #3.)</td></tr>
<tr><td rowspan="2">*Incorrect response*</td><td rowspan="2">***/mmm/. Say /mmm/.***</td><td>*Correct*</td><td>**Good.**</td><td>(Present practice item #3.)</td></tr>
<tr><td>*Incorrect*</td><td>***Okay.***</td><td>(Present practice item #3.)</td></tr>
</table>

Practice item #3) ***Let's try another word, "sun."*** (Wait up to 3 seconds for student to respond.) If the student does not respond, ask, ***What is the first sound you hear in the word "sun"?***

<table>
<tr><td>*Correct response*
/sss/ or /su/</td><td>***Good. /sss/ is the first sound in "sun."***</td><td>(Begin testing.)</td></tr>
</table>

<table>
<tr><td rowspan="3">*Incorrect response*
Student does not respond within 3 <u>seconds</u> or responds <u>incorrectly</u></td><td rowspan="3">***/sss/ is the first sound you hear in the word "sun." Listen. /sss/. "Sun." Say it with me. /sss/. Let's try it again. What is the first sound you hear in the word "sun"?***</td><td>*Correct response*</td><td>**Good.**</td><td colspan="3">(Begin testing.)</td></tr>
<tr><td rowspan="2">*Incorrect response*</td><td rowspan="2">***/sss/. Say /sss/.***</td><td>*Correct*</td><td>**Good.**</td><td>(Begin testing.)</td></tr>
<tr><td>*Incorrect*</td><td>***Okay.***</td><td>(Begin testing.)</td></tr>
</table>

Begin testing. ***Now I am going to say more words. You tell me the first sound you hear in the word.***

---

1. Say the first word and start your stopwatch.
2. During the testing:
   - Present the words to the student one at a time by reading down the column of words.
   - Score the student's responses by circling the corresponding sound or group of sounds on the scoring page. Mark a slash (/) through the zero for no response or for an incorrect response.
   - As soon as the student finishes saying the initial sound/sounds in the word, say the next word promptly and clearly.
   - Continue to say the words one at a time and score the student's responses for 1 minute.
   - At the end of **1 minute**, stop presenting the words. Do not score any student responses after 1 minute. If the student completes the assessment before 1 minute, stop testing and record the score obtained. Scores are not prorated.

3. Immediately after testing:
   - Reset the stopwatch for the next measure.
   - Make a note in the scoring booklet about any patterns in student responses that were not captured by the marking procedures.
4. At a later time (i.e., shortly after the testing when you are no longer with the student) compute the final score:
   - Add the correct responses in the 2-point column. Multiply the number of responses from the 2-point column by two and record the total in the space provided.
   - Add the correct responses in the 1-point column and record the total in the space provided.
   - Add the two totals from each column together and record the total score in the space provided.
   - Record the score on the front of the scoring booklet.

Scoring Rules

Scoring Rules

The student receives 2 points for correctly identifying the initial phoneme in isolation and 1 point for identifying the correct initial sounds (consonant blend, consonant plus vowel, or consonant blend plus vowel).

1. Circle the corresponding sound or sounds that a student says for a word. A response is scored as correct if the student says any of the responses listed for the word.
   - A student receives 2 points by correctly identifying the initial phoneme in a word.
   - A student receives 1 point for identifying the correct initial consonant blend, consonant plus vowel, or consonant blend plus vowel in a word.
2. Mark a slash (/) through the zero on the scoring page for an incorrect response or no response within 3 seconds.
3. Write "sc" over the slash and circle the corresponding sounds or group of sounds in the student's response if the student self-corrects an error within 3 seconds.

Discontinue Rule

Discontinue Rule

Discontinue administering FSF if the student has not said any correct initial sounds in the first five words. Record a score of 0 on the Total line on the scoring page and in the FSF score box on the cover page of the student booklet.

Wait Rule

Wait Rule

Wait 3 seconds for the student to respond. If the student does not respond within 3 seconds on a word, mark a slash (/) through the zero and say the next word.

Reminders

Reminders

If you think the student may have forgotten the task (e.g., the student stops responding because he or she has clearly forgotten the task, repeats the word, claps the sounds, or says a rhyming word), say ***Remember***

to tell me the <u>first</u> sound that you hear in the word. Immediately say the next word. *This reminder may be given as often as needed.*

If the student says the name of the letter, say ***Remember to tell me the first <u>sound</u> in the word, not the letter name.*** Immediately say the next word. *This reminder may be given only once.*

Notes:

1. Schwa sounds (/u/) added to consonants are not counted as errors. Some phonemes (e.g., voiced phonemes such as /g/ or /b/) cannot be pronounced in isolation without a vowel, and some early learning of sounds includes the schwa.
2. Students are not penalized for differences in pronunciation due to dialect, articulation delays or impairments, or for speaking a first language other than English. It is common for preschool and kindergarten children to say /ch/ for /tr/ and /j/ for /dr/. On FSF, these substitutions are considered articulation errors and are scored as correct.

Examples of Scoring Rules

The following are examples of how to score commonly occurring responses on FSF. Please pay attention to the notes included with the examples as they provide scoring explanations and indicate variations and nuances related to the scoring. The examples do not encompass all possible responses. If in doubt about how to score a student response, refer to the scoring rules above.

Correct Response

Scoring Rule 1: Circle the corresponding sound or sounds that a student says for a word. A response is scored as correct if the student says any of the responses listed for the word.

Examples:

Words fish, drop — ***Student response*** /f/ or /fu/, /d/ or /du/

How to score

Test Items	Correct/2 points	Correct/1 point	Incorrect
1. fish	(/f/) circled	/fi/	0
2. drop	(/d/) circled	/dr/ /dro/	0

Note: Schwa sounds (/u/) added to consonants are not counted as errors.

Words fish, drop — ***Student response*** /fi/, /dr/ or /dru/

How to score

Test Items	Correct/2 points	Correct/1 point	Incorrect
1. fish	/f/	(/fi/) circled	0
2. drop	/d/	(/dr/) circled /dro/	0

Note: Schwa sounds (/u/) added to consonants are not counted as errors.

Correct Response (cont.)

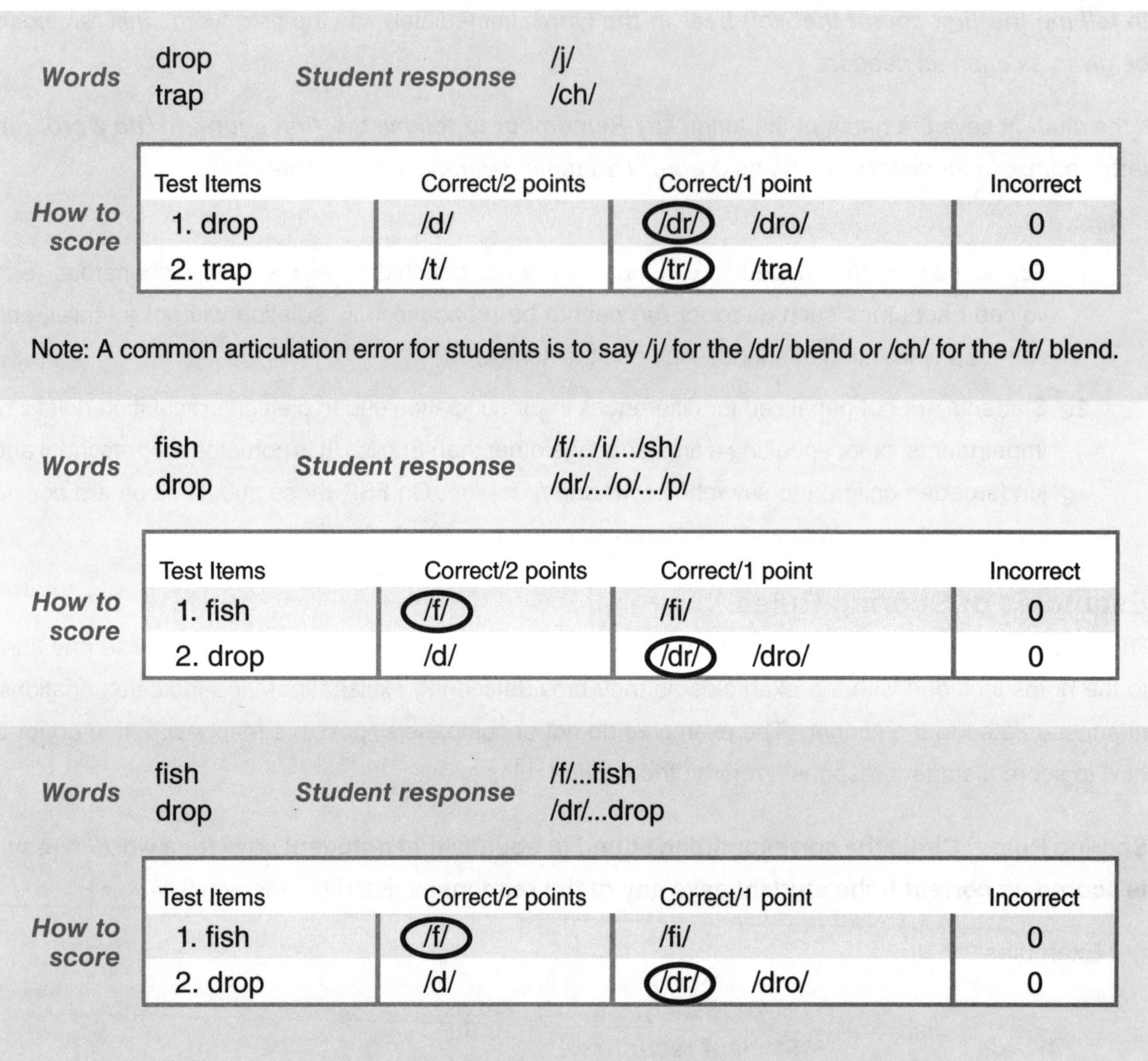

Words drop, trap — **Student response** /j/, /ch/

How to score

Test Items	Correct/2 points	Correct/1 point		Incorrect
1. drop	/d/	/dr/	/dro/	0
2. trap	/t/	/tr/	/tra/	0

Note: A common articulation error for students is to say /j/ for the /dr/ blend or /ch/ for the /tr/ blend.

Words fish, drop — **Student response** /f/.../i/.../sh/, /dr/.../o/.../p/

How to score

Test Items	Correct/2 points	Correct/1 point		Incorrect
1. fish	/f/	/fi/		0
2. drop	/d/	/dr/	/dro/	0

Words fish, drop — **Student response** /f/...fish, /dr/...drop

How to score

Test Items	Correct/2 points	Correct/1 point		Incorrect
1. fish	/f/	/fi/		0
2. drop	/d/	/dr/	/dro/	0

Incorrect Sounds

Scoring Rule 2: **Mark a slash (/) through the zero for no response or for any other response not included on the score sheet (e.g., incorrect sound, letter name, repeat the word).**

Examples:

Words fish, drop — **Student response** /m/, drop

How to score

Test Items	Correct/2 points	Correct/1 point		Incorrect
1. fish	/f/	/fi/		~~0~~
2. drop	/d/	/dr/	/dro/	~~0~~

Words fish, drop — **Student response** eff...(assessor says, "Remember to tell me the first sound in the word, not the letter name. Drop.")...dee...

How to score

Test Items	Correct/2 points	Correct/1 point		Incorrect
1. fish	/f/	/fi/		~~0~~
2. drop	/d/	/dr/	/dro/	~~0~~

Note: This reminder may be used only once.

Words fish, drop — **Student response** no response...(3 seconds)...(assessor says, "drop") /dr/

How to score

Test Items	Correct/2 points	Correct/1 point		Incorrect
1. fish	/f/	/fi/		~~0~~
2. drop	/d/	(/dr/)	/dro/	0

Note: Slash the zero if the student gives no response after 3 seconds.

Scoring Rule 3: **Write "sc" over the slashed zero if the student self-corrects. Circle the appropriate score for the student's response.**

Self-correction

Examples:

Words fish, drop — **Student response** /m/...I mean /f/ drop...I mean /d/

How to score

Test Items	Correct/2 points	Correct/1 point		Incorrect
1. fish	(/f/)	/fi/		SC ~~0~~
2. drop	(/d/)	/dr/	/dro/	SC ~~0~~

See Appendix 2, pages 117 and 118, for Practice Scoring Sheet and Answer Key.

FSF Scoring Sheet

Model FSF Scoring Sheet

The following is an example of a completed scoring sheet. The scoring rules and scoring calculation are shown. This scoring sheet serves as a model and can be used during training and practice to support accurate administration and scoring of *DIBELS*.

1 DIBELS® First Sound Fluency

Test Items	Correct/2 points	Correct/1 point		Incorrect
1. knob	/n/	/no/		0
2. jam	/j/	/ja/		0
3. throat	/th/	/thr/	/throa/	0
4. slow	/s/	/sl/		0
5. shelves	/sh/	/she/		0
6. slice	/s/	/sl/	/slie/	0
7. time	/t/	/tie/		0
8. sports	/s/	/sp/	/spor/	0
9. chance	/ch/	/cha/		0
10. plot	/p/	/pl/	/plo/	0
11. skate	/s/	/sk/	/skai/	0
12. sand	/s/	/sa/		0
13. dropped	/d/	/dr/	/dro/	0
14. loud	/l/	/low/		0
15. storm	/s/	/st/	/stor/	sc 0
16. peak	/p/	/pea/		0
17. smash	/s/	/sm/	/sma/	0
18. tree	/t/	/tr/		0
19. fair	/f/	/fe/		0
20. dad	/d/	/da/		0
21. smooth	/s/	/sm/	/smoo/	0
22. clean	/k/	/kl/	/klea/	0
23. cheer	/ch/	/chi/		0
24. nine	/n/	/nie/		0
25. space	/s/	/sp/	/spai/	0
26. dirt	/d/	/der/		0
27. creek	/k/	/kr/	/krea/	0
28. zoom	/z/	/zoo/		0
29. call	/k/	/ko/		0
30. scarf	/s/	/sk/	/skar/	0

2-pt responses: 17

x 2: 34 + 1-pt responses: 10 = Total: 44

Basic Early Literacy Skill	*DIBELS* Indicator
Not directly linked to a basic early literacy skill	Letter Naming Fluency

What is letter naming?

To read an alphabetic writing system such as English, students must be able to recognize letters, name the letters, and associate the letters with their corresponding sounds (Troia, 2004). However, letter naming is not one of the five core components of early literacy. Many, though not all, students enter kindergarten with some knowledge of letter names. Many can sing the alphabet song and can recite the names of the letters in a sequence. Surrounded by environmental print, many students can easily recognize the letter shapes and print cues of their favorite stores or foods. All these experiences provide an entry point to the printed word.

The pragmatic implication of having learned letter names through rhythm and song is that teaching the visual representation for each letter follows easily and almost naturally. The value of recognizing environmental print is that students begin to understand that print has meaning. The importance of knowing letter names in mastering the alphabetic principle is ambiguous because the skill of knowing the alphabet letter names is not essential to reading outcomes. Nevertheless, knowledge of letter names in kindergarten is a strong and robust predictor of later reading performance (Adams, 1990), and has an enduring relationship with phonological awareness (Kaminski & Good, 1996; Scarborough, 1998; Stahl & Murray, 1994; Wagner, Torgesen, & Rashotte, 1994).

Chapter 6: ***DIBELS*** Letter Naming Fluency (LNF)

Overview

Basic Early Literacy Skill	None
Administration Time	1 minute
Administration Schedule	Beginning of kindergarten to beginning of first grade
Score	Number of letters named correctly in 1 minute
Wait Rule	If the student does not name a letter within 3 seconds, mark a slash (/) through the letter and say the correct letter name.
Discontinue Rule	No letters named correctly in the first row

What is LNF?

Letter Naming Fluency (LNF) is a brief, direct measure of a student's fluency in naming letters. LNF assesses a student's ability to recognize individual letters and say their letter names. Using standardized directions, the assessor presents a page of uppercase and lowercase letters arranged in random order and asks the student to name the letters. The assessor marks letter names that are read incorrectly or skipped. The total score is the number of correct letter names that the student says in 1 minute.

The purpose of LNF is to measure students' automaticity with letter naming. Fluency in naming letters is a strong and robust predictor of later reading achievement (Adams, 1990). The purpose of LNF is to measure fluency rather than identify which letters the student knows or does not know, so while all letters are included on the LNF materials, they appear in random order. As such, it provides an added risk indicator for early school-age children. Although it may be related to rapid automatized naming (RAN), it is not a measure of RAN.

Because letter naming does not appear to be essential for achieving reading outcomes, it is not a basic early literacy skill. Therefore, a benchmark goal is not provided. As an indicator of risk, scores on Letter Naming Fluency should be used in conjunction with scores on other measures, especially at the beginning of kindergarten. LNF is a strong and robust predictor of later reading achievement but is not a powerful instructional target, i.e., focusing instruction on letter names should not be expected to lead to better reading outcomes. For students at risk, the primary instructional goals should be developing phonological awareness skills and gaining knowledge about the alphabetic principle.

Materials

- Scoring Booklet
- Assessment Book
- Pen/pencil
- Clipboard
- Stopwatch

Administration Directions

Follow these directions exactly each time with each student. Say the words in bold italic type verbatim. Begin with the practice activities. The practice activities are designed to introduce the assessment task to the student. They are untimed and include correction procedures. The correction procedures are not used once the testing begins. Put the student copy of the materials in front of the student and say the following:

▶ ***I am going to show you some letters. I want you to point to each letter and say its name.*** (Put the page of letters in front of the student.)

▶ **Begin testing.** ***Start here*** (point to the first letter at the top of the page)***. Go this way*** (sweep your finger across the first two rows of letters) ***and say each letter name. Put your finger under the first letter*** (point)***. Ready, begin.***

1. Start your stopwatch after you say ***begin.***
2. During the testing:
   - Follow along in the scoring booklet. Mark a slash (/) through any skipped letter or letter read incorrectly.
   - At the end of **1 minute**, put a bracket after the last letter named and tell the student to ***Stop***. If the student completes the assessment before 1 minute, stop testing and record the student's score. Scores are not prorated.
3. Immediately after testing:
   - Reset the stopwatch for the next measure.
   - Mark LNF response patterns and make a note in the scoring booklet about any patterns in student responses that were not captured by the marking procedures.
4. At a later time (shortly after testing but when you are no longer with the student) compute the final score:
   - Add the number of correct letters and record the number on the Total line of the LNF scoring page.
   - Record the score on the front page of the scoring booklet.

Scoring Rules

Scoring Rules

The student receives 1 point for each letter correctly named in 1 minute.

1. Do not mark letters named correctly. Young students sometimes confuse the lowercase L with uppercase I. Give the student a point for naming the lowercase L as either an L or an I. Do not give the student a point for calling it a number 1.

2. Mark a slash (/) through any letter the student names incorrectly, skips, or does not name within 3 seconds.

3. Write "sc" above any letter that had been previously slashed and was self-corrected within 3 seconds. Count the self-corrected response as correct.

4. Draw a line through any row the student skips. Do not count the row when scoring.

Discontinue Rule

Discontinue Rule

Discontinue administering LNF if the student does not correctly name any letters in the first row. Tell the student to ***Stop.*** Record a score of 0 on the Total line on the scoring page and in the LNF score box on the cover page of the student booklet.

Wait Rule

Wait Rule

Wait 3 seconds for the student to respond. If the student does not name a letter within 3 seconds, mark a slash (/) through the letter and say the correct letter name.

Reminders

Reminders

If the student names letters from top to bottom, or points randomly, say ***Go this way.*** (Sweep your finger across the row). *This reminder may be given only once.*

If the student skips four or more consecutive letters, but does not skip the whole row, say ***Try to say each letter name.*** *This reminder may be given only once.*

If the student says letter sounds rather than letter names, say ***Say the letter name, not its sound.*** If the student continues saying letter sounds, mark each letter as incorrect and indicate the pattern of response at the bottom of the page. *This reminder may be given only once.*

If the student stops and it is not a hesitation on a specific item, say ***Keep going.*** *This reminder may be used as often as needed.*

If the student loses his/her place, point. *This reminder may be used as often as needed.*

Note:

Students are not penalized for differences in pronunciation due to dialect, articulation delays or impairments, or speaking a first language other than English.

Examples of Scoring Rules

The following are examples of how to score responses on LNF. Please pay attention to the notes included with the examples as they provide scoring explanations and indicate variations and nuances related to the scoring. The examples do not encompass all possible responses. If in doubt about how to score a student response, refer to the scoring rules on page 55.

Correct Response

Scoring Rule 1: Do not mark any letter the student names correctly.

Example:

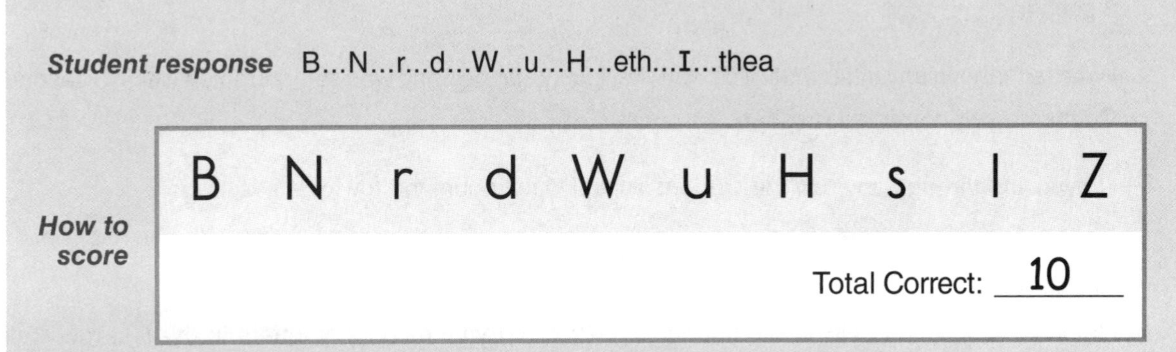

Notes: (1) In the font used on LNF, the lowercase L may look like an uppercase I. Give the student a point for naming the lowercase L as either an L or an I. Do not give the student a point for calling it a number 1. (2) Students are not penalized for differences in pronunciation due to dialect, articulation delays or impairments, or for pronunciations due to speaking a first language other than English.

Incorrect Response

Scoring Rule 2: Mark a slash (/) through any letter the student names incorrectly, skips, or does not name within 3 seconds.

Example:

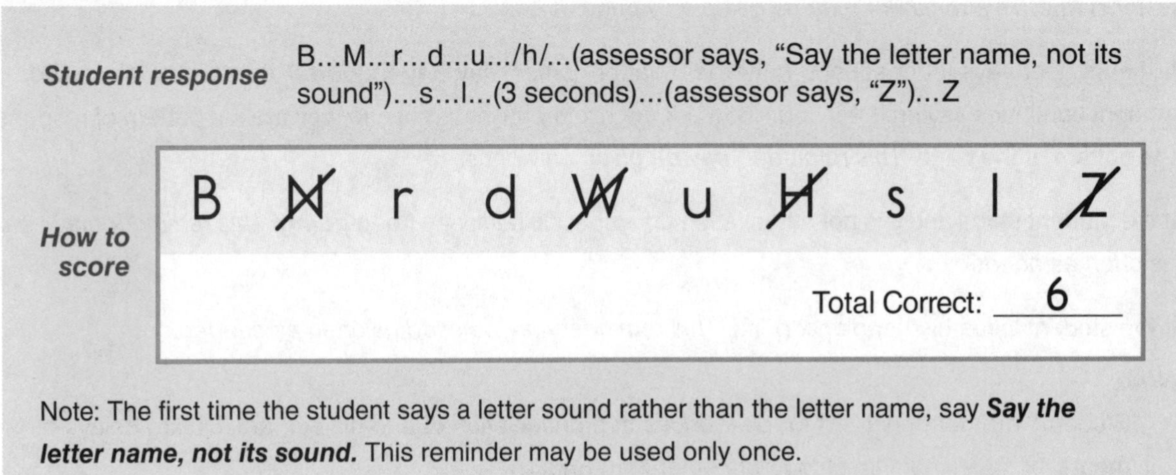

Note: The first time the student says a letter sound rather than the letter name, say ***Say the letter name, not its sound.*** This reminder may be used only once.

Self-correction

Scoring Rule 3: **Write "sc" above any letter that had been previously slashed and was self-corrected within 3 seconds. Count the self-corrected response as correct.**

Example:

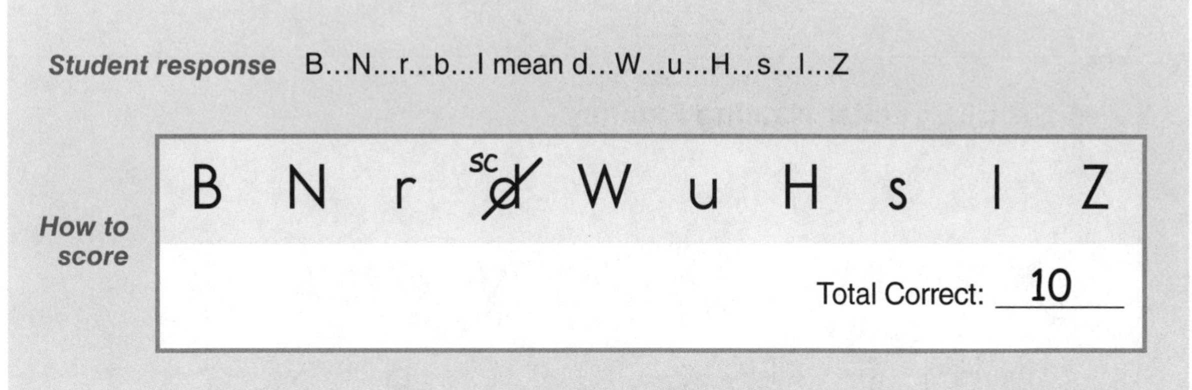

Tracking

Scoring Rule 4: **Draw a line through any row the student skips.**

Example:

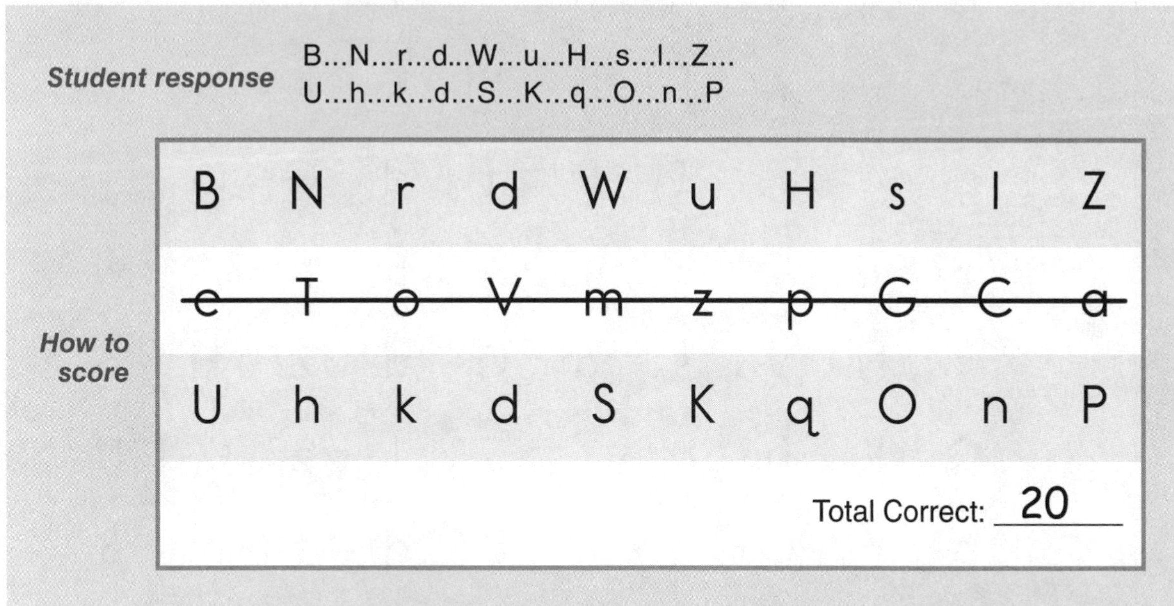

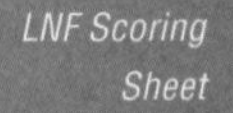

Model LNF Scoring Sheet

The following is an example of a completed scoring sheet. The scoring rules and scoring calculation are shown. This scoring sheet serves as a model and can be used during training and practice to support accurate administration and scoring of *DIBELS*.

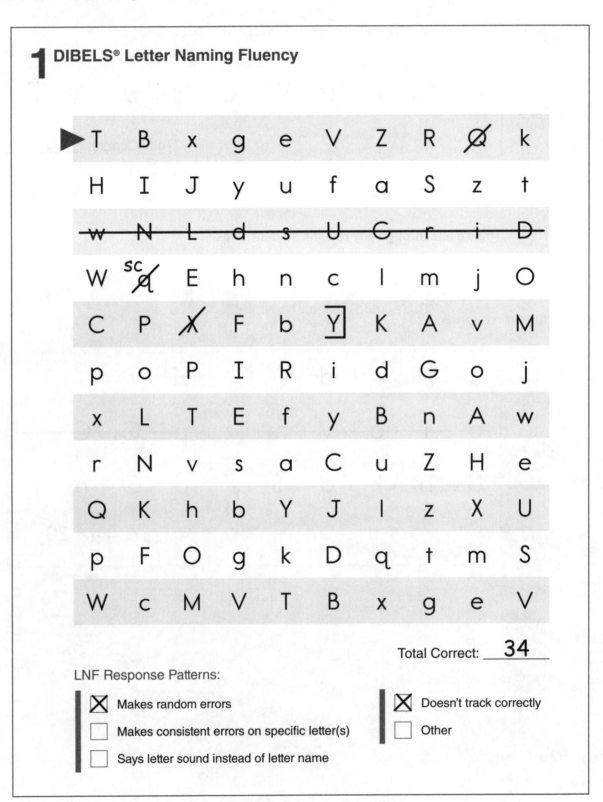

1 DIBELS® Letter Naming Fluency

▶T	B	x	g	e	V	Z	R	~~O~~	k
H	I	J	y	u	f	a	S	z	t
~~w~~	~~N~~	~~L~~	~~d~~	~~s~~	~~U~~	~~G~~	~~r~~	~~i~~	~~D~~
W	~~q~~ sc	E	h	n	c	l	m	j	O
C	P	~~X~~	F	b	Y]	K	A	v	M
p	o	P	I	R	i	d	G	o	j
x	L	T	E	f	y	B	n	A	w
r	N	v	s	a	C	u	Z	H	e
Q	K	h	b	Y	J	l	z	X	U
p	F	O	g	k	D	q	t	m	S
W	c	M	V	T	B	x	g	e	V

Total Correct: 34

LNF Response Patterns:

- [x] Makes random errors
- [ ] Makes consistent errors on specific letter(s)
- [ ] Says letter sound instead of letter name
- [x] Doesn't track correctly
- [ ] Other

Basic Early Literacy Skill	*DIBELS* Indicator
Phonemic Awareness	Phoneme Segmentation Fluency

What is phonemic awareness?

Phonemic awareness is the explicit awareness that spoken words are made up of individual sounds or phonemes. A phoneme is the smallest sound unit into which speech can be divided that makes a difference to the meaning of the word (National Reading Panel, 2000). Phonemic awareness involves the ability to attend to and manipulate these phonemes in spoken words. For example, the knowledge that the word *dog* begins with the sound /d/ is phonemic awareness. The ability to replace the /d/ sound at the beginning of *dog* with the /h/ sound to make the word *hog* is also phonemic awareness. Phonemic awareness is an auditory skill that does not require knowledge of the letters of the alphabet or letter-sound knowledge, thus it is not the same as phonics.

A convergence of research on the acquisition of reading skills has demonstrated that phonemic awareness is highly predictive of success in learning to read (Gillon, 2004; Stahl & Murray, 2006). Additionally, effective instruction in phonemic awareness leads to significant differences in reading achievement (Ehri, 2004; National Reading Panel, 2000). Most reading researchers advocate that phonemic awareness be purposefully and explicitly taught as part of a comprehensive instructional program in reading and writing.

Chapter 7: **DIBELS Phoneme Segmentation Fluency (PSF)**

Overview

Basic Early Literacy Skill	Phonemic Awareness
Administration Time	1 minute
Administration Schedule	Middle of kindergarten to beginning of first grade
Score	Number of correct sound segments (different, correct parts of the words) the student says in 1 minute
Wait Rule	If the student does not respond within 3 seconds, say the next word.
Discontinue Rule	Zero correct sound segments in the first five words

What is PSF?

Phoneme Segmentation Fluency (PSF) is a brief, direct measure of phonemic awareness. PSF assesses the student's fluency in segmenting a spoken word into its component parts or sound segments. Using standardized directions, the assessor says a word and asks the student to say the sounds in the word. The assessor underlines each correct sound segment of the word that the student says. *Appendix 1*, page 115, provides a pronunciation guide for how individual sounds are represented on the PSF measure. A correct sound segment is any different, correct part of the word the student says. The total score is the number of correct sound segments that the student says in 1 minute. For example, if the assessor says the word *fish* and the student says /f/ /i/ /sh/, the student has completely and correctly segmented the word into its component sounds and the score is 3 correct sound segments. If the student says /f/ /ish/, the score is 2 correct sound segments.

Partial credit is given for partial segmentation. A student who is developing phonemic awareness may not yet segment words completely into individual sounds but *may* segment parts of words. For example, a student who says the first sound of the word *sun* (/s/) receives 1 point. A student who says the onset and rime (/s/ /un/) receives 2 points and a student who completely and correctly segments all of the individual phonemes in the word (/s/ /u/ /n/) receives 3 points. Note that consonant blends have two or more phonemes that should be produced separately for a student to receive full credit. For example, for the word *trap*, a student who says /tr/ /a/ /p/ receives partial credit of 3 points, and a student who says /t/ /r/ /a/ /p/ receives the full 4 points. Allowing partial credit in scoring increases the sensitivity of the measure, thus making it possible to measure growth from partial to complete segmentation. Although partial credit is given, the preferred response is for students to completely segment words at the phoneme level by the end of kindergarten.

Materials

- Scoring Booklet
- Pen/pencil
- Stopwatch
- Assessment Book
- Clipboard

Administration Directions

Administration Directions

Follow these directions exactly each time with each student. Say the words in bold italic type verbatim. Begin with the practice activities. The practice activities are designed to introduce the assessment task to the student. They are untimed and include correction procedures. The correction procedures are not used once the testing begins.

▶ ***We are going to say the sounds in words. Listen to me say all the sounds in the word "fan." /f/ /a/ /n/. Listen to another word,*** (pause) ***"jump." /j/ /u/ /m/ /p/. Your turn. Say all the sounds in "soap."***

Correct response /s/ /oa/ /p/	***Very good saying all the sounds in "soap."***	(Begin testing.)

Incorrect response anything other than /s/ /oa/ /p/	***I said "soap," so you say /s/ /oa/ /p/. Your turn. Say all the sounds in "soap."***	*Correct response*	***Good.***	(Begin testing.)
		Incorrect response	***Okay.***	(Begin testing.)

▶ **Begin testing.** ***I am going to say more words. I will say the word, and you say all the sounds in the word.*** (Say the first word from the list in the scoring booklet.)

1. Say the first word and start your stopwatch.
2. During the testing:
   - Present the words to the student one at a time by reading across the row.
   - As the student responds, underline each correct sound segment the student says. A sound segment is defined as each different, correct part of the word. Leave omitted sounds blank. Circle repeated words.
   - As soon as the student finishes saying the sounds of the word, say the next word promptly and clearly. If the student indicates that he/she did not hear the word, you may repeat it.
   - Continue to say words one at a time and score the student's responses for 1 minute.

- At the end of **1 minute**, put a bracket after the last sound segment the student said. Stop presenting words and do not score any student responses after 1 minute. If the student is in the middle of a response at the end of 1 minute, you may allow the student to finish his/her response, but place the bracket where the minute ended and do not count any sound segments after the end of the minute. If the student completes the assessment before 1 minute, stop testing and record the student's score. Scores are not prorated.

3. Immediately after testing:
   - Reset the stopwatch for the next measure.
   - Mark PSF Response Patterns and make a note in the scoring booklet about any patterns in student responses that were not captured by the marking procedures.
4. At a later time (shortly after the testing but when you are no longer with the student) compute the final score:
   - Add the number of correct sound segments (i.e., underlined parts of words) for each row and record the number in the space provided at the right side of each row.
   - Add the number of correct sound segments from all rows and record the total number on the Total line of the PSF scoring page.
   - Record the score on the cover page.

Scoring Rules

The student receives 1 point for each different, correct sound segment produced in 1 minute.

1. Underline each correct sound segment the student says. A correct sound segment is any correct *part* of the word. To be correct, the sound segment must be a correct part of the word in its entirety. For example, /m/ /ma/ /a/ /an/ /n/ are all correct parts of the word *man*. /mae/ is not a correct part of the word *man* even though it contains /m/. Blended sounds or partial segmentation should be underlined exactly as the student said the sounds, and given 1 point per underline.
2. Mark a slash (/) through any incorrect sound segment. Score the entire sound segment as correct or incorrect.
3. Circle the word if the student repeats the word without saying any sound segments.
4. Leave blank any sounds the student omits.
5. Write "sc" over any corrected sound segments that had previously been slashed if the student self-corrects an error within 3 seconds.

Discontinue Rule

Discontinue Rule

Discontinue administering PSF if the student has not said any correct sound segments in the first five words. Record a score of 0 for the total number of correct sound segments on the Total line on the scoring page and in the PSF score box on the cover page of the student booklet.

Wait Rule

Wait Rule

Wait 3 seconds for the student to respond. If the student does not respond within 3 seconds, say the next word.

Reminders

Reminders

If the student spells the word, say ***Say the sounds in the word.*** Immediately say the next word. *This reminder may be given only once.*

If the student repeats the word, say ***Remember to say all the sounds in the word.*** Immediately say the next word. *This reminder may be given only once.*

Notes:

1. Schwa sounds (/u/) added to consonants are not counted as errors. Some phonemes cannot be pronounced correctly in isolation without a vowel, and some early learning of sounds includes the schwa.
2. Students may elongate the individual sounds and get credit if you judge that they have awareness of each individual sound in the word (e.g., they have held each sound for approximately 1 second).
3. Students are not penalized for differences in pronunciation due to dialect, articulation delays or impairments, or speaking a first language other than English.

Examples of Scoring Rules

The following are examples of how to score responses on PSF. The examples do not encompass all possible responses. If in doubt about how to score a student response, refer to the scoring rules above. Please pay attention to the notes included with the examples as they provide scoring explanations and indicate variations and nuances related to the scoring.

Scoring Rule 1: Underline each correct sound segment a student says. Correct sound segments are different, correct parts of the word. Blended sounds or partially correct segments should be underlined exactly as the student said them, and 1 point given per underline.

Examples:

Words	***Student response***	***How to score***	Score
flag	/f/.../l/.../a/.../g/	flag /f/ /l/ /a/ /g/	4 /4
sit	/s/.../i/.../t/	sit /s/ /i/ /t/	3 /3

Note: The student completely segments the words at the individual phoneme level.

Words	Student response	How to score	Score
flag	/f/	flag /f/ /l/ /a/ /g/	1 /4
flag	/fla/.../g/	flag /f/ /l/ /a/ /g/	2 /4
sit	/s/.../it/	sit /s/ /i/ /t/	2 /3

Note: The student says only some of the sounds in the word or combines sounds. The student does not receive credit for sound segments that are not said.

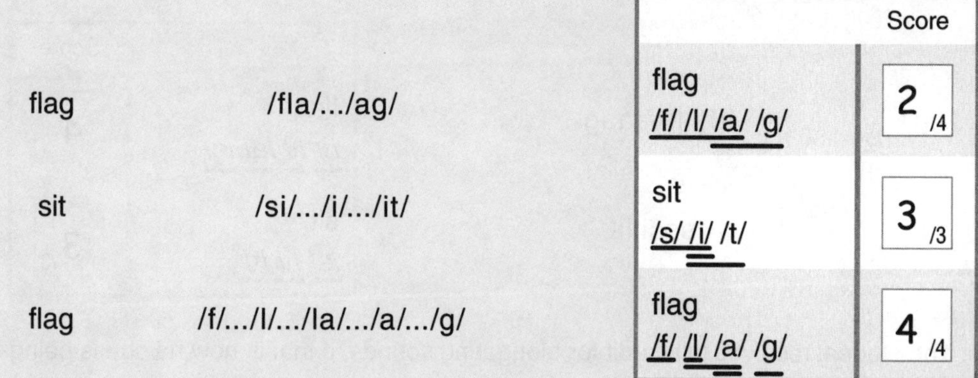

Words	Student response	How to score	Score
flag	/fla/.../ag/	flag /f/ /l/ /a/ /g/	2 /4
sit	/si/.../i/.../it/	sit /s/ /i/ /t/	3 /3
flag	/f/.../l/.../la/.../a/.../g/	flag /f/ /l/ /a/ /g/	4 /4

Note: If the student repeats a sound in adjacent segments, the student receives credit as long as each segment is a different, correct part of the word. The student cannot receive more points for a word than the maximum number of phonemes in the word. This is an uncommon response pattern, and not as desirable as /f/ /l/ /a/ /g/.

Correct Sounds (cont.)

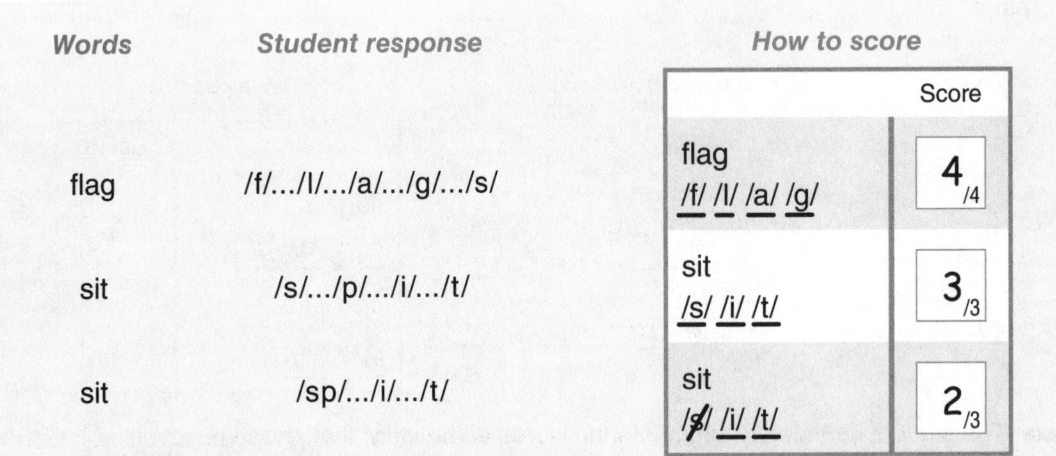

Words	Student response	How to score	Score
flag	/f/.../l/.../a/.../g/.../s/	flag /f/ /l/ /a/ /g/	4 /4
sit	/s/.../p/.../i/.../t/	sit /s/ /i/ /t/	3 /3
sit	/sp/.../i/.../t/	sit ~~/s/~~ /i/ /t/	2 /3

Note: Added sounds are disregarded in scoring if they are separated from the other sounds in the word. If a student consistently adds sounds to words, make a note and follow up to determine why this is happening.

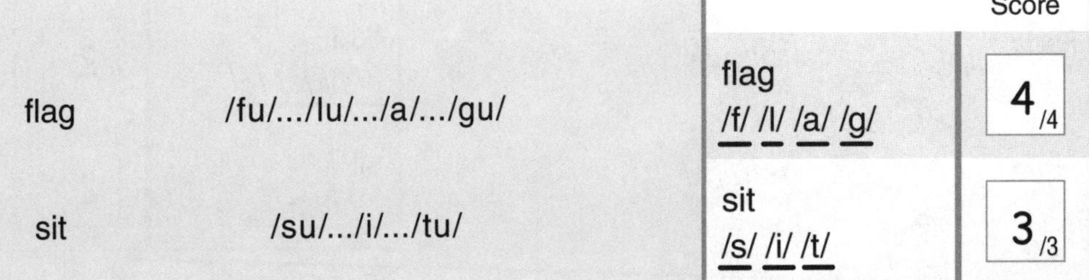

Words	Student response	How to score	Score
flag	/fu/.../lu/.../a/.../gu/	flag /f/ /l/ /a/ /g/	4 /4
sit	/su/.../i/.../tu/	sit /s/ /i/ /t/	3 /3

Note: Schwa sounds (/u/) added to a sound are not counted as errors. If a student consistently adds the schwa sound, make a note.

Words	Student response	How to score	Score
flag	ffffllllaaaag	flag /f/ /l/ /a/ /g/	4 /4
sit	ssssiiiit	sit /s/ /i/ /t/	3 /3

Note: The student receives full credit for elongating sounds, if that is how he/she is being taught to segment sounds in words, and the assessor judges that the student demonstrates awareness of each individual sound in the word.

Words	Student response	How to score	Score
flag	/f/.../w/.../a/.../g/	flag /f/ /l/ /a/ /g/	4 /4
this	/d/.../i/.../s/	this /TH/ /i/ /s/	3 /3

Note: There is no penalty for articulation errors or dialect differences when assessing a student. For example, a student with an articulation delay who consistently says /w/ for /l/ would not be penalized for this pronunciation. A student who speaks a dialect and consistently says /d/ for /TH/ would not be penalized for this pronunciation. Many other examples of articulation errors and dialect differences are possible.

Incorrect Sounds

Scoring Rule 2: **Mark a slash (/) through any incorrect sound segment. Score the entire sound segment as correct or incorrect.**

Examples:

Words	Student response	How to score	Score
flag	/f/.../l/.../a/.../p/	flag /f/ /l/ /a/ /g/ (slash through /g/)	3 /4
sit	/s/.../if/.../t/	sit /s/ /i/ /t/ (slash through /i/)	2 /3

Note: The sound segment is judged in its entirety to be correct or incorrect. For example, if the word is *sit* and the student says, "/s/.../if/.../t/," mark a slash through the /i/ because there is no /if/ sound in the word *sit*.

Repetition

Scoring Rule 3: Circle the word if the student repeats the word without providing any sound segments.

Examples:

Words	*Student response*	*How to score*	Score
flag	flag	flag (/f/ /l/ /a/ /g/) circled	0 /4
sit	sit	sit (/s/ /i/ /t/) circled	0 /3
flag	/f/...flag	flag (/f/ /l/ /a/ /g/) circled, /f/ underlined	1 /4

Note: If the student says a sound segment and then repeats the entire word, underline the corresponding sound(s) and circle the word. The student receives credit for any correct sound segments.

No Response

Scoring Rule 4: Leave blank any omitted sounds.

Examples:

Words	*Student response*	*How to score*	Score
flag	/f/.../l/.../g/	flag /f/ /l/ /a/ /g/ (/f/, /l/, /g/ underlined)	3 /4
sit	/s/.../t/	sit /s/ /i/ /t/ (/s/, /t/ underlined)	2 /3

Self-correction

Scoring Rule 5: **Write "sc" over any corrected sound segments that had previously been slashed if the student self-corrects an error within 3 seconds.**

Examples:

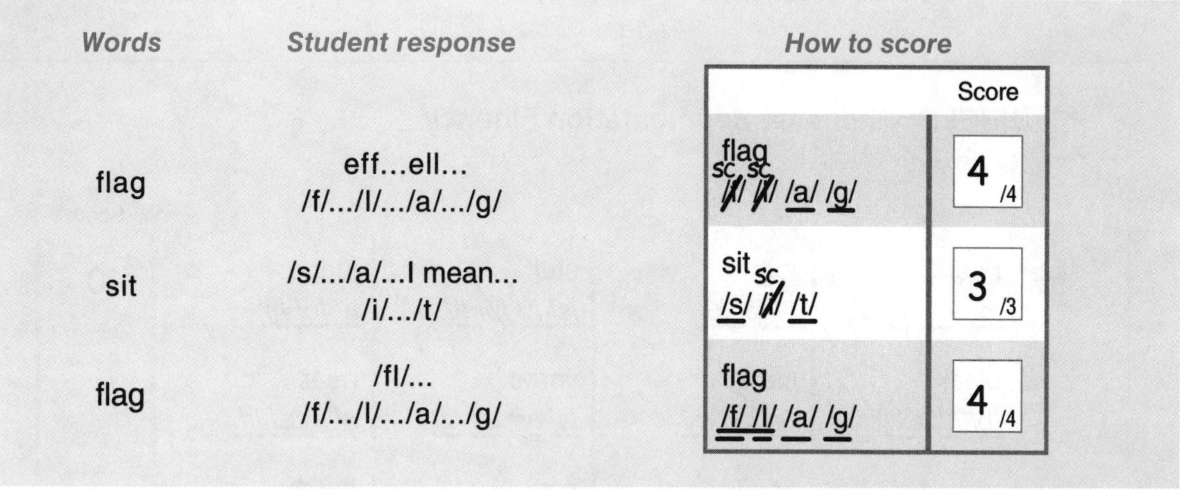

Words	Student response	How to score	Score
flag	eff...ell... /f/.../l/.../a/.../g/	flag sc sc /f/ /l/ /a/ /g/	4 /4
sit	/s/.../a/...I mean... /i/.../t/	sit sc /s/ /i/ /t/	3 /3
flag	/fl/... /f/.../l/.../a/.../g/	flag /f/ /l/ /a/ /g/	4 /4

See Appendix 2, pages 119 and 120, for Practice Scoring Sheet and Answer Key.

PSF Scoring Sheet

Model PSF Scoring Sheet

The following is an example of a completed scoring sheet. The scoring rules and scoring calculation are shown. This scoring sheet serves as a model and can be used during training and practice to support accurate administration and scoring of *DIBELS*.

3 DIBELS® Phoneme Segmentation Fluency

				Score
boat /b/ /oa/ /t/	log /l/ /o/ /g/	stuff /s/ /t/ /u/ /f/	judge /j/ /u/ /j/	10 /13
black /b/ /l/ /a/ /k/	cane /k/ /a/ /n/ (sc)	verbs /v/ /ir/ /b/ /z/	near /n/ /ea/ /r/	11 /14
run /r/ /u/ /n/	seeds /s/ /ea/ /d/ /z/	have /h/ /a/ /v/	much /m/ /u/ /ch/	10 /13
clue /k/ /l/ /oo/	wet /w/ /e/ /t/	met /m/ /e/ /t/	new /n/ /oo/	9 /11
hill /h/ /i/ /l/	groups /g/ /r/ /oo/ /p/ /s/	knife /n/ /ie/ /f/	bill /b/ /i/ /l/	6 /14
shake /sh/ /ai/ /k/	plane /p/ /l/ /ai/ /n/	own /oa/ /n/	ball /b/ /o/ /l/	/12

Total: 46

PSF Response Patterns:

- [ ] Repeats word
- [ ] Makes random errors
- [ ] Says initial sound only
- [ ] Says onset rime
- [ ] Does not segment blends
- [ ] Adds sounds
- [ ] Makes consistent errors on specific sound(s)
- [x] Other some difficulty on vowel sounds and ending sounds

Basic Early Literacy Skills	*DIBELS* Indicator
Alphabetic Principle and Basic Phonics	Nonsense Word Fluency ◆ Correct Letter Sounds ◆ Whole Words Read

What are the alphabetic principle and basic phonics?

In order for students to learn how to read in an alphabetic writing system, they must first be able to map individual speech sounds to symbols. In the case of written English, these symbols are letters. Unlocking the reading code begins when associations are made between letters and sounds.

The alphabetic principle is comprised of two parts:

- *Alphabetic understanding:* Knowledge of letter-sound correspondences and the understanding that letters represent sounds in spoken words.
- *Phonological recoding:* The use of alphabetic understanding to decode or read unknown words.

Phonics is the system of letter-sound relationships that is the foundation for decoding words in print. Phonics skills must be explicitly taught and practiced (Ehri, 1991; Liberman & Liberman, 1990). A student's understanding of the alphabetic principle and basic phonics begins first by using letter-sound correspondences to segment and then blend simple CVC words, or to retrieve these correspondences to spell a word.

It is the automaticity with the sequences of letter sounds comprising frequent words and spelling patterns that enables skillful readers to process text quickly and easily (Adams, 1990). Development of the alphabetic principle and basic phonics is essential for decoding unknown words (Adams, 1990; Ehri, 2002) and for developing the sight-word vocabulary necessary for fluent reading (Share, 1995; Share & Stanovich, 1995).

Chapter 8: *DIBELS* Nonsense Word Fluency (NWF)

Overview

Basic Early Literacy Skills	Alphabetic Principle and Basic Phonics
Administration Time	1 minute
Administration Schedule	Middle of kindergarten to beginning of second grade
Scores	• Number of correct letter sounds (CLS) • Number of whole words read (WWR) without sounding out
Wait Rule	If the student responds sound-by-sound, mixes sounds and words, or sounds out and recodes, allow 3 seconds, then provide the correct letter sound. If the student responds with whole words, allow 3 seconds, then provide the correct word.
Discontinue Rule	No correct letter sounds in the first row

What is NWF?

Nonsense Word Fluency (NWF) is a brief, direct measure of the alphabetic principle and basic phonics. It assesses knowledge of basic letter-sound correspondences and the ability to blend letter sounds into consonant-vowel-consonant (CVC) and vowel-consonant (VC) words. The test items used for NWF are phonetically regular make-believe (nonsense or pseudo) words. To successfully complete the NWF task, students must rely on their knowledge of letter-sound correspondences and how to blend sounds into whole words. One reason that nonsense word measures are considered to be a good indicator of the alphabetic principle is that "pseudo-words have no lexical entry, [and thus] pseudo-word reading provides a relatively pure assessment of students' ability to apply grapheme-phoneme knowledge in decoding" (Rathvon, 2004, p. 138).

Following a model and a practice item, the student is presented with a sheet of randomly ordered VC and CVC nonsense words (e.g., *dif*, *ik*, *nop*). Standardized directions are used to ask the student to read the make-believe words the best they can, reading either the whole word or saying any sounds they know. For example, if the stimulus word is *tof,* the student could say /t/ /o/ /f/ or "tof." The assessor underlines each correct letter sound produced either in isolation or blended together. Whole words read without sounding out are underlined in their entirety.

There are two separate scores reported for NWF:

1. Correct Letter Sounds (CLS) is the number of letter sounds produced correctly in 1 minute. For example, if the student reads dif as /d/ /i/ /f/ the score for Correct Letter Sounds is 3. If the student reads *dif* as /di/ /f/ or "dif," the score is also 3.
2. Whole Words Read (WWR) is the number of make-believe words read correctly as a whole word without first being sounded out. For example, if the student reads *dif* as "dif," the score is 3 points for CLS and 1 point for WWR, but if the student reads *dif* as "/d/ /i/ /f/ dif," the score is 3 points for CLS but 0 points for WWR.

The goal is for students to read whole words on NWF; however, an advantage of NWF is that it allows for monitoring the development of the alphabetic principle and basic phonics as early as the middle of kindergarten, when producing individual letter sounds is the more common response.

Materials

- Scoring Booklet
- Assessment Book
- Pen/pencil
- Clipboard
- Stopwatch

Administration Directions

Follow these directions exactly each time with each student. Say the words in bold italic type verbatim. Begin with the practice activities. The practice activities are designed to introduce the assessment task to the student. They are untimed and include correction procedures. The correction procedures are not used once the testing begins. Put the student copy of the materials in front of the student and say the following:

▶ ***We are going to read some make-believe words. Listen. This word is "sog."*** (Run your finger under the word as you say it.) ***The sounds are /s/ /o/ /g/*** (point to each letter)***. Your turn. Read this make-believe word*** (point to the word "mip")***. If you can't read the whole word, tell me any sounds you know.***

<table>
<tr><td>Correct Whole Word Read
mip</td><td colspan="3">Very good reading the word "mip."</td><td>(Begin testing.)</td></tr>
<tr><td>Correct Letter Sounds
Any other response with all the correct letter sounds</td><td colspan="3">Very good. /m/ /i/ /p/ (point to each letter) or "mip" (run your finger under the word as you say it).</td><td>(Begin testing.)</td></tr>
<tr><td rowspan="2">Incorrect response
No response within 3 <u>seconds</u>, or response includes any errors</td><td rowspan="2">Listen. /m/ /i/ /p/ or "mip." (Run your finger under the letters as you say the sounds.) Your turn. Read this make-believe word. (Point to the word "mip.") If you can't read the whole word, tell me any sounds you know.</td><td>Correct response</td><td>Very good.</td><td>(Begin testing.)</td></tr>
<tr><td>Incorrect response</td><td>Okay.</td><td>(Begin testing.)</td></tr>
</table>

▶ **Begin testing.** ***I would like you to read more make-believe words. Do your best reading. If you can't read the whole word, tell me any sounds you know.*** (Place the student copy in front of the student.) ***Put your finger under the first word. Ready, begin.***

1. Start the stopwatch after you say ***begin***.
2. During the testing:
   - Underline each correct letter sound the student says either in isolation or blended together. Use separate underlines to indicate reading sound-by-sound and a continuous underline to indicate blending together two or three sounds.
   - Mark a slash (/) through any letter sound read incorrectly.
   - At the end of **1 minute**, place a bracket after the last letter sound produced (even if it's in the middle of a nonsense word), say ***Stop***, and stop the stopwatch. If the student completes the assessment before 1 minute, stop testing and record the student's score. Scores are not prorated.
3. Immediately after testing:
   - Reset the stopwatch for the next measure.

- Make a note in the scoring booklet about any patterns in student responses that were not captured by the marking procedures.

4. At a later time (shortly after the testing when you are no longer with the student) compute the final score:
   - Record the total number of correct letter sounds (CLS) on the Total Correct Letter Sounds line of the NWF scoring page.
   - Record the total number of whole words read correctly (WWR) on the Total Whole Words Read line of the NWF scoring page.
   - Record each score in the appropriate box on the front page of the scoring booklet.

Scoring Rules

Scoring Rules

Correct Letter Sounds (CLS): The student receives credit for 1 CLS for each correct letter sound read in isolation or read as part of a make-believe word.

Whole Words Read (WWR): The student receives credit for 1 WWR for each whole word read correctly without first being sounded out.

1. Underline each letter sound the student says correctly, either in isolation or blended with other sounds in the word. For CLS, score the student's final answer. For WWR, give credit only if the student's first and only answer was to read the whole word correctly without first sounding it out.
2. Mark a slash (/) through any incorrect letter sound.
3. Leave blank any omitted letter sounds or words. When a student is reading sound-by-sound, leave blank any inserted letter sounds. When the student is reading word-by-word, slash the underline to indicate any inserted letter sounds.
4. Write "sc" above any letter sound that had been previously slashed and was self-corrected within 3 seconds. Count that letter sound as correct. Credit is given for WWR only when the student reads the whole word completely and correctly the first time, and reads the word only once.
5. Draw a line through any row the student skips. Do not count the row when scoring.

Discontinue Rule

Discontinue Rule

Discontinue administering NWF if the student has not said any correct letter sounds in the first row. Record a score of 0 on the Total line on the scoring page and in the NWF score box on the cover page of the student booklet.

Wait Rule

Wait Rule

Wait 3 seconds for the student to respond. If the student has been responding sound-by-sound, mixing sounds and words, or by sounding out and recoding, allow 3 seconds, then provide the correct letter sound. If the student has been responding by reading the words as whole words, allow 3 seconds, then provide the correct word.

If the student hesitates in the middle of a word, wait 3 seconds, then provide the correct letter sound.

If providing the correct letter sound or word does not prompt the student to continue, say ***Keep going.***

Reminders

Reminders

If the student does not read from left to right, say ***Go this way***. (Sweep your finger across the row.) *This reminder may be given only once.*

If the student says letter names, say ***Say the sounds, not the letter names***. *This reminder may be given only once.*

If the student reads the word first, then says the letter sounds, say ***Just read the word***. *This reminder may be given only once.*

If the student says all of the letter sounds correctly in the first row, but does not attempt to blend or recode, say ***Try to read the words as whole words***.

If the student stops (and it's not a hesitation on a specific item), say ***Keep going***. *This reminder may be used as often as needed.*

If the student loses his/her place, point. *This reminder may be used as often as needed.*

Notes:

1. Schwa sounds (/u/) added to consonants are not counted as errors when the student is saying letter sounds. Some phonemes cannot be pronounced correctly in isolation without a vowel, and some early learning of sounds includes the schwa.
2. Students are not penalized for differences in pronunciation due to dialect, articulation delays or impairments, or speaking a first language other than English.

Examples of Scoring Rules

The following are examples of how to score responses on NWF. The examples do not encompass all possible responses. If in doubt about how to score a student response, refer to the scoring rules on the previous page. Please pay attention to the notes included with the examples as they provide scoring explanations and indicate variations and nuances related to the scoring.

Correct Response

Scoring Rule 1: **Underline each letter sound the student says correctly, either in isolation or blended with other sounds in the word. For CLS, score the student's final answer. For WWR, give credit only if the student's first and only answer was to read the whole word correctly without first sounding it out.**

Examples:

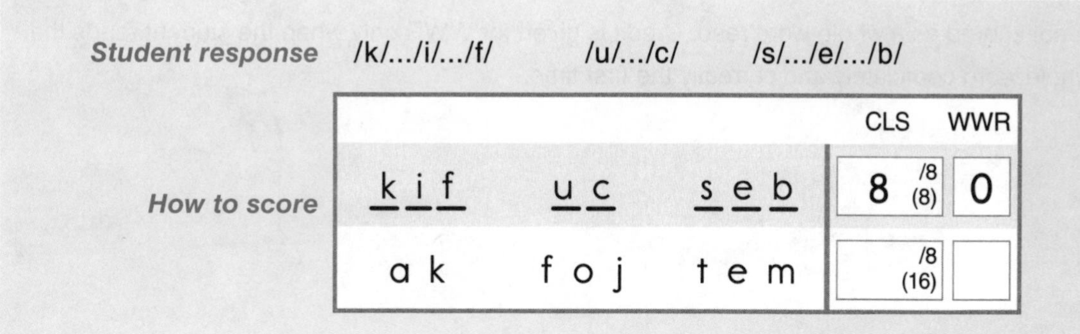

				CLS	WWR
Student response	/k/.../i/.../f/	/u/.../c/	/s/.../e/.../b/		
How to score	<u>k</u> <u>i</u> <u>f</u>	<u>u</u> <u>c</u>	<u>s</u> <u>e</u> <u>b</u>	8 /8 (8)	0
	a k	f o j	t e m	/8 (16)	

Correct Response (cont.)

Note: Use separate underlines under each correct sound if the student correctly says the letter sounds in isolation but does not recode the sounds into words.

Student response kif uc seb

How to score

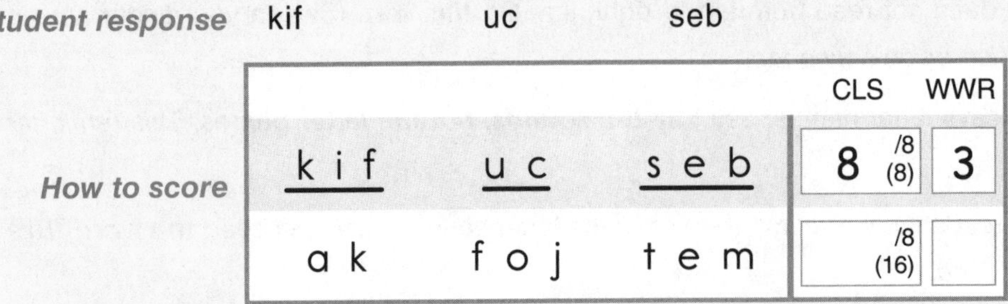

CLS WWR
k i f u c s e b
8 /8 (8) 3
a k f o j t e m
/8 (16)

Note: Use a continuous underline under all of the sounds if the student says all of the correct letter sounds and says them as a whole word.

Student response /k/.../if/ /u/.../c/ /se/.../b/

How to score

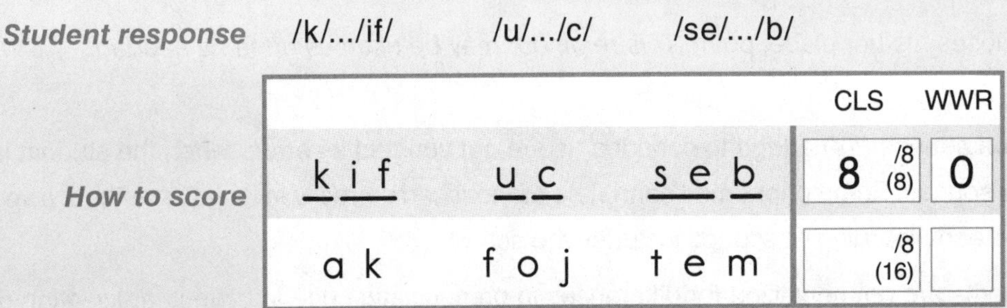

Note: Underline exactly the way the student says the sounds for partially blended words.

Student response /k/.../i/.../f/...kif /u/.../c/...uc /s/.../eb/...seb

How to score

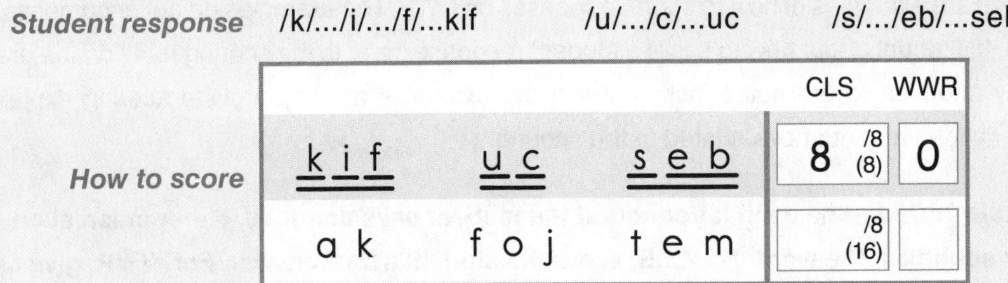

Note: Indicate exactly the way the student reads the word, even if multiple rows of underlines are required. Score the student's final answer for CLS. This pattern is sounding out and recoding, and is not scored as a whole word read. Credit is given for WWR only when the student reads the whole word completely and correctly the first time.

Student response /k/.../i/.../k/.../if/.../kif/
/u/.../uc/
/seb/.../seb/

How to score

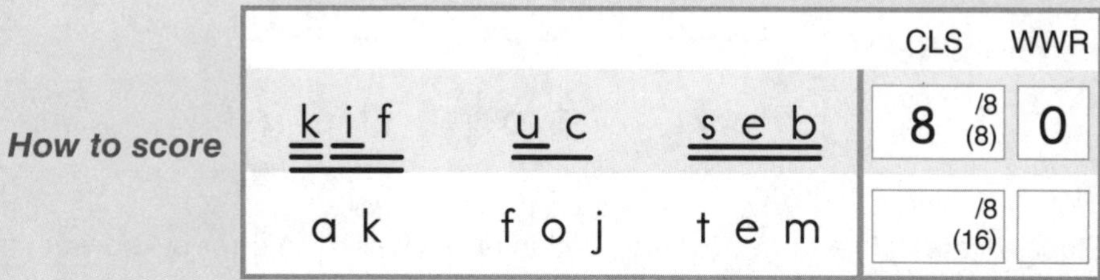

Note: If the student repeats the letter sounds while sounding out a word, show it with multiple underlines but give credit for each sound only once. To receive a point for WWR, the student must read the whole word correctly the first time, and read the word only once.

Student response /f/.../i/.../k/ (student points correctly)
/c/.../u/ (student points correctly)
/b/.../e/.../s/ (student doesn't point correctly)

How to score

			CLS	WWR
k i f	u c	s e b (s and b slashed)	6 /8 (8)	0
a k	f o j	t e m	/8 (16)	

Note: Letter sounds said correctly in isolation but out of order are scored as correct ***if the student points correctly*** to the letter(s). The purpose of this rule is to give students credit as they are beginning to learn individual letter-sound correspondences.

Student response fik cu bes

How to score

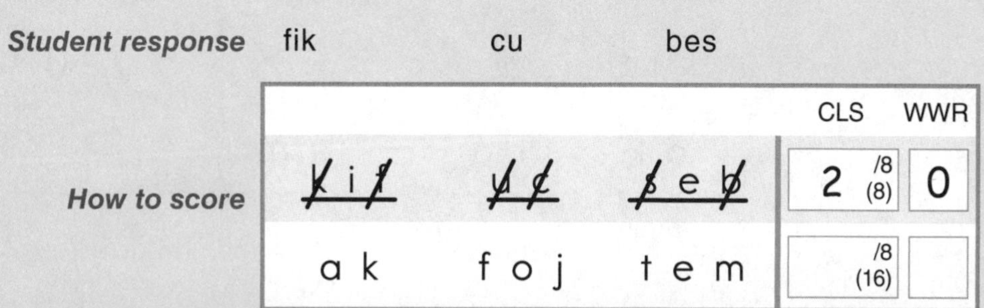

Note: Blended sounds must be in the correct position to receive credit. Give credit if the medial vowel is produced correctly, even within a word with other incorrect sounds. No credit is given for WWR. Although the sounds were blended together, they were not in the correct order.

Correct Response (cont.)

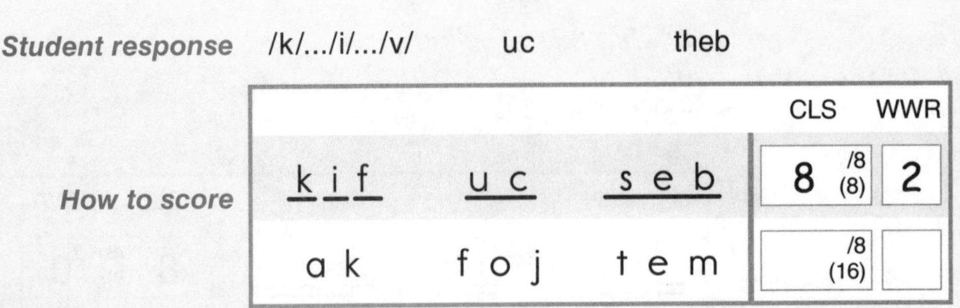

Student response /k/.../i/.../v/ uc theb

How to score

			CLS	WWR
k i f	u c	s e b	8 /8 (8)	2
a k	f o j	t e m	/8 (16)	

Note: Students are not penalized for articulation errors when the error is known to the assessor and is part of the student's typical speech. If in doubt, score it as incorrect. If necessary, have the student retested by someone familiar with his/her speech or articulation pattern.

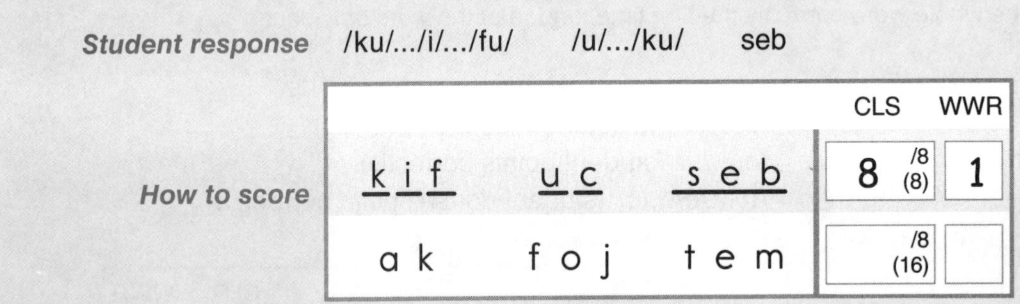

Student response /ku/.../i/.../fu/ /u/.../ku/ seb

How to score

			CLS	WWR
k i f	u c	s e b	8 /8 (8)	1
a k	f o j	t e m	/8 (16)	

Note: Students are not penalized for putting a schwa sound after consonants.

Incorrect Response

Scoring Rule 2: Mark a slash (/) through any incorrect letter sound.

Examples:

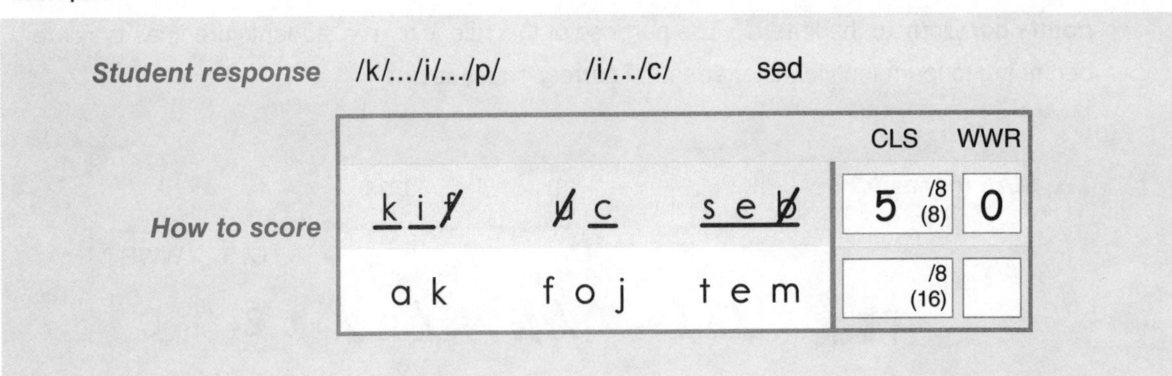

Student response /k/.../i/.../p/ /i/.../c/ sed

How to score

			CLS	WWR
k i ~~f~~	~~u~~ c	s e ~~b~~	5 /8 (8)	0
a k	f o j	t e m	/8 (16)	

Student response /k/.../ie/.../f/ /u/.../s/ seab

How to score

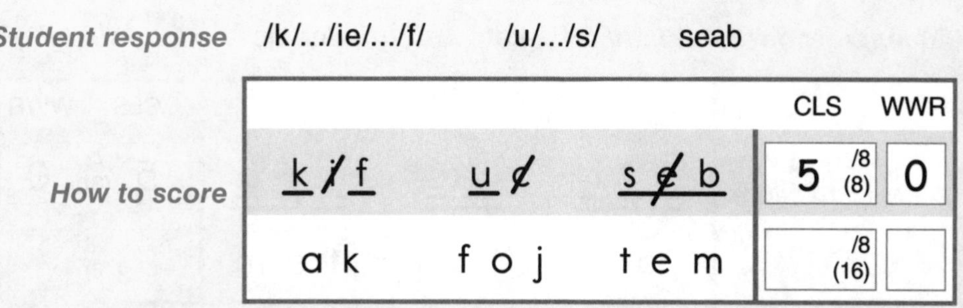

			CLS	WWR
k i f	u c	s e b	5 /8 (8)	0
a k	f o j	t e m	/8 (16)	

Note: The student gets credit for saying the most common sound for each letter according to basic phonics rules. Vowels should be pronounced with the short vowel sound.

Student response
/k/...(3 seconds)...(assessor says, "/i/")…/f/
/u/.../c/
/s/.../e/...(3 seconds)...(assessor says, "/b/")…/b/

How to score

			CLS	WWR
k i f	u c	s e b	6 /8 (8)	0
a k	f o j	t e m	/8 (16)	

Note: If the student is reading individual letter sounds and hesitates for more than 3 seconds, provide the letter sound and mark it as incorrect.

Student response kif...(3 seconds)...(assessor says, "uc")...seb

How to score

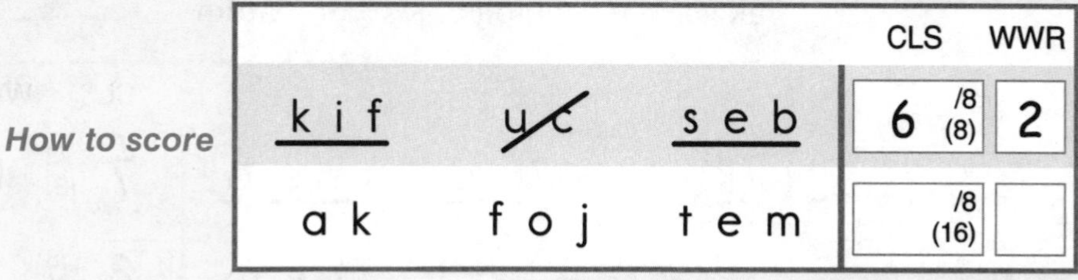

			CLS	WWR
k i f	u c	s e b	6 /8 (8)	2
a k	f o j	t e m	/8 (16)	

Note: If the student is reading whole words and hesitates for more than 3 seconds, provide the word and score it as incorrect. Mark a slash through any letters or words that were told to the student because they were not read within 3 seconds.

Incorrect Response (cont.)

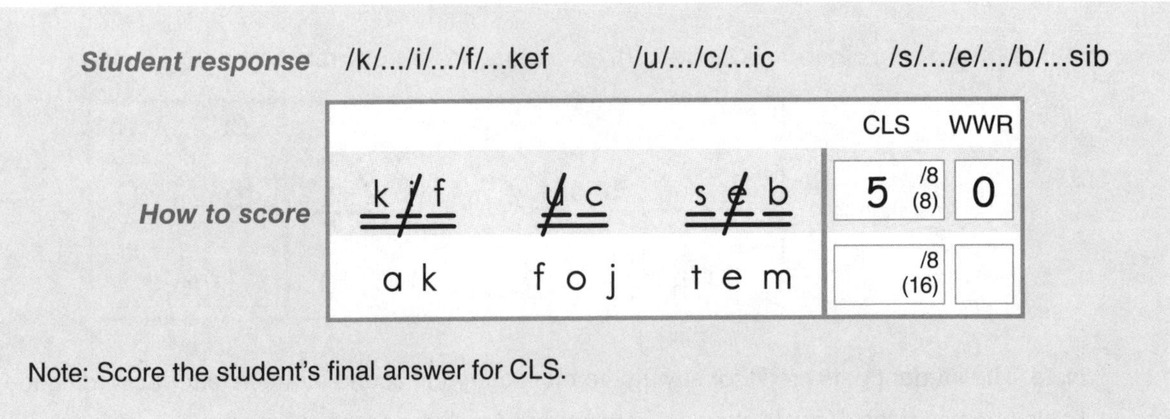

Omitted/ added sounds

Scoring Rule 3: **Leave blank any omitted letter sounds or words. When a student is reading sound-by-sound, leave blank any inserted letter sounds. When the student is reading word-by-word, slash the underline to indicate any inserted letter sounds.**

Examples:

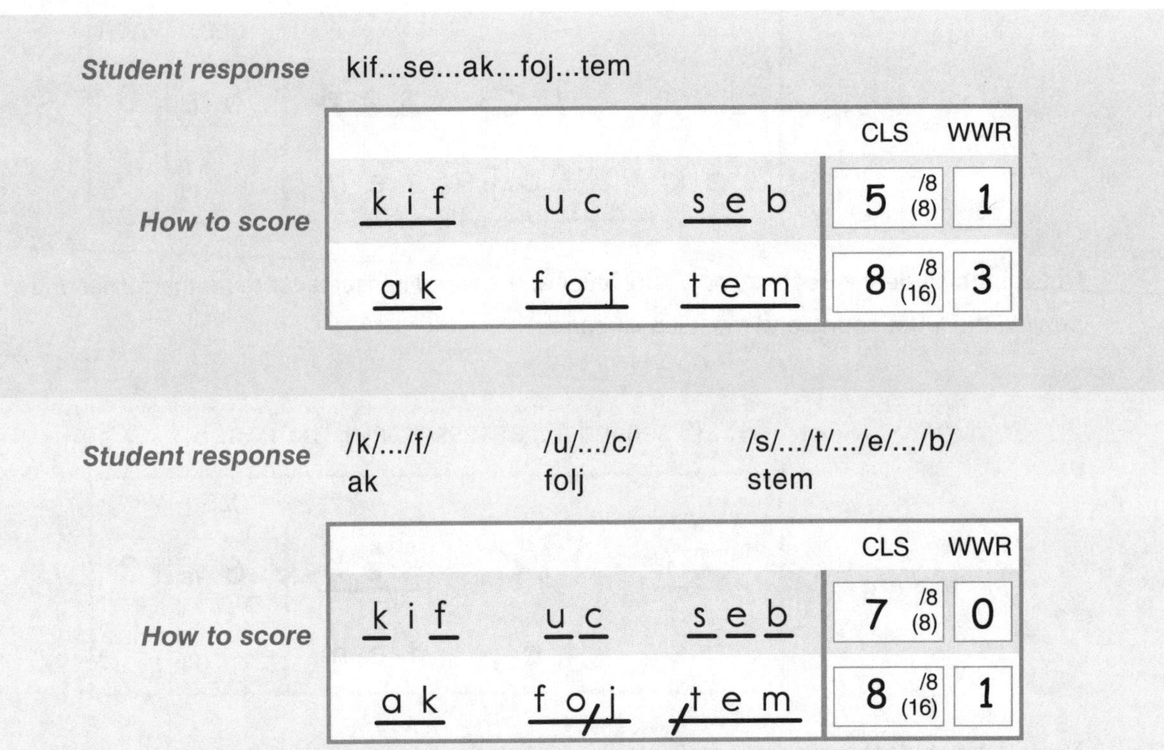

Note: Leave blank any inserted sounds. If inserting sounds is a frequent response, make a note in the margin of the student scoring booklet. No credit is given for WWR when a sound is inserted. Put a slash through the underline to indicate inserted sounds when the student is reading word-by-word.

Scoring Rule 4: **Write "sc" above any letter sound that had been previously slashed and was self-corrected within 3 seconds. Count that letter sound as correct. No credit is given for WWR unless the student reads the whole word completely and correctly the first time, and reads the word only once.**

Examples:

Student response /k/.../e/.../f/...I mean /k/.../i/.../f/
ic...uc
sed...I mean...seb

How to score

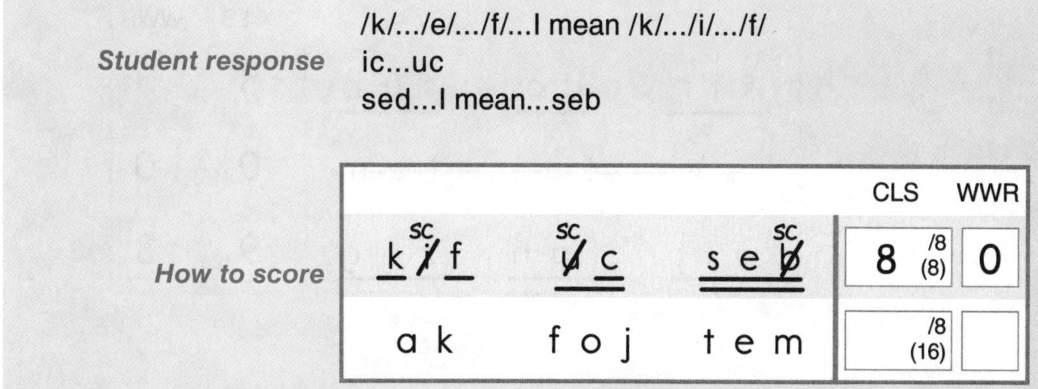

Note: Give students credit on CLS for self-corrects within 3 seconds.

Student response /k/.../e/.../f/...kif /oo/.../c/...uc /s/.../i/.../b/...seb

How to score

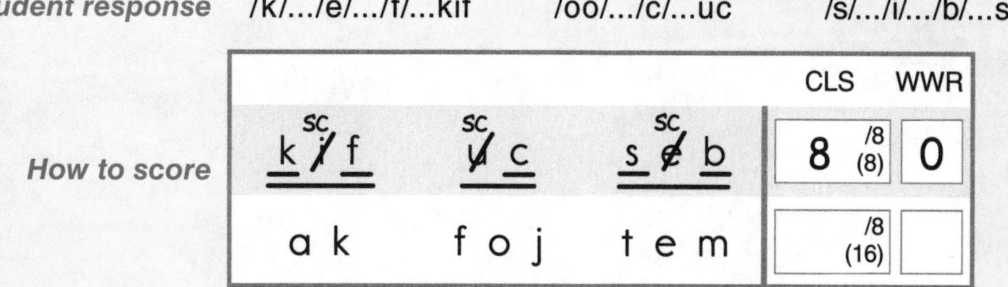

Note: Score the student's final answer for CLS. If the word is not read completely and correctly the first time, then no credit is given for WWR.

Tracking

Scoring Rule 5: Draw a line through any row the student skips. Do not count the row when scoring.

Example:

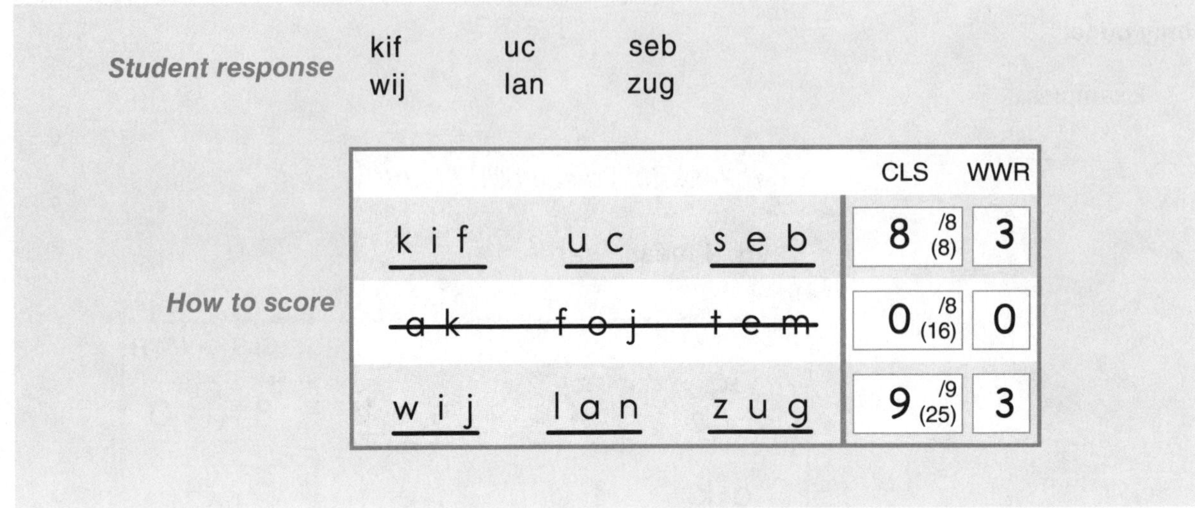

See Appendix 2, pages 121 and 122, for Practice Scoring Sheet and Answer Key.

Model NWF Scoring Sheet

The following is an example of a completed scoring sheet. The scoring rules and scoring calculation are shown. This scoring sheet serves as a model and can be used during training and practice to support accurate administration and scoring of *DIBELS*.

3 DIBELS® Nonsense Word Fluency

					CLS	WWR
▶ bac	roz	em	wut	dil	14 /14 (14)	1
poj	kip	zed	uj	hap	14 /14 (28)	2
vez	sig	jok	nod	duv	14 /15 (43)	1
en	fuj	zop	ras	tik	13 /14 (57)	3
ag	wic]	nol	neg	kuz	4 /14 (71)	1
kek	viv	dod	pav	juc	/15 (86)	
mus	av	wec	miv	dop	/14 (100)	
tac	liz	vul	fos	eg	/14 (114)	
dif	tov	zez	nus	wan	/15 (129)	
jad	ob	hiz	mek	num	/14 (143)	

Total Correct Letter Sounds (CLS): 59

Total Whole Words Read (WWR): 8

NWF Response Patterns:

- ☐ Says correct sounds out of order (sound-by-sound)
- ☐ Makes random errors
- ☐ Says correct sounds, does not recode
- ☐ Says correct sounds, recodes out of order
- ☐ Says correct sounds, recodes with incorrect sound(s)
- ☐ Says correct sounds and correctly recodes
- ☐ Doesn't track correctly
- ☐ Tries to turn nonsense words into real words
- ☐ Makes consistent errors on specific letter sound(s)
- ☐ Other

Basic Early Literacy Skills	*DIBELS* Indicator
Advanced Phonics and Word Attack Skills	*DIBELS* Oral Reading Fluency ◆ Accuracy
Accurate and Fluent Reading of Connected Text	*DIBELS* Oral Reading Fluency ◆ Correct Words Per Minute ◆ Accuracy
Reading Comprehension	*DIBELS* Oral Reading Fluency ◆ Correct Words Per Minute ◆ Retell Total/Quality of Response

What are advanced phonics and word attack skills?

Advanced phonics skills are an extension of basic phonics skills such as letter-sound correspondence and decoding of simple letter patterns and syllables. Advanced phonics includes skills such as recognizing common sounds related to combinations of letters (e.g., digraphs, blends, vowel teams, trigraphs), understanding the way the position of the letter(s) in a syllable or word affects the sound, and knowledge of affixes. Word attack skills are the approach to pronouncing and knowing the meaning of a word through the application of phonics, the use of context, and knowledge of morphology. Advanced phonics and word attack skills facilitate the accurate and automatic reading of connected text.

What is accurate and fluent reading of connected text?

Accuracy and fluency with connected text, both critical components of skilled reading, allow meaning to be gained from text. To read a text easily and make sense of it, a large percentage of the words must be decoded effortlessly (Ehri, 1998). Reading fluency depends on well-developed word attack skills (National Reading Panel, 2000), efficient and automatic decoding of regular and irregular words, and the use of expression and phrasing while reading aloud (Dowhower, 1991; Schreiber, 1987, 1991). Oral reading fluency in connected text is more than the accurate reading of words in lists and is not speed-reading. Oral reading fluency can be described as the bridge between accurate, automatic, word-level decoding and reading comprehension.

What is reading comprehension?

Reading comprehension represents the ultimate goal of instruction in the other basic early literacy skills. It is a complex collection of skills that includes accurate and fluent reading, monitoring while reading, and the ability to use cognitive strategies flexibly to gain meaning from text (Goldman & Rakestraw, 2000; Pressley, 2000). While reading comprehension is dependent on decoding skills, decoding skills by themselves are not enough (Adams, 1990). In addition to decoding, reading comprehension requires access to linguistic knowledge about syntax, semantics, and word morphology (Catts & Kahmi, 1999; McGuinness, 2005); prior knowledge about words in a given context (Duke, Pressley & Hilden, 2004); and reasoning skills. It is only through the skillful interplay of both bottom-up decoding skills and top-down meaning-making skills that the student reads for meaning.

What is the relationship between oral reading fluency and reading comprehension?

The relationship between oral reading fluency and reading comprehension is strong and complex and has been extensively researched (Crowder & Wagner, 1992; LaBerge & Samuels, 1974; Perfetti, 1985; Wolf & Katzir-Cohen, 2001). While a recognized relationship between oral reading fluency and comprehension exists, more research will further illuminate the nature of the reciprocal relationship. Reading fluency by itself is not sufficient for comprehension. Vocabulary and language knowledge also play a direct role in reading comprehension, and overall vocabulary instruction does improve comprehension (Stahl & Fairbanks, 1986). On the other hand, well-developed vocabulary and oral language skills by themselves are also not sufficient for reading comprehension. The student also must access the text fluently and automatically.

Chapter 9: ***DIBELS*** **Oral Reading Fluency (DORF)**

Overview

Basic Early Literacy Skills	Advanced Phonics and Word Attack Skills Accurate and Fluent Reading of Connected Text Reading Comprehension
Administration Time	1 minute plus 1 minute maximum for Retell
Administration Schedule	Middle of first grade through end of sixth grade
Scores	• Median number of words correct per minute (Words Correct) • Median number of errors per minute (Errors) • Median number of correct words in the Retell • Median Quality of Response for the Retell
Wait Rule	On DORF, 3 seconds; On Retell, first hesitation 3 seconds
Discontinue Rule	If no words are read correctly in the first line, say ***Stop***, record a score of 0, and do not administer Retell. If fewer than 10 words are read correctly on passage #1 during benchmark assessment, do not administer Retell or passages #2 and #3. If fewer than 40 words are read correctly on any passage, use professional judgment whether to administer Retell for that passage.

What is DORF?

DIBELS Oral Reading Fluency (DORF) is a measure of advanced phonics and word attack skills, accurate and fluent reading of connected text, and reading comprehension. The DORF passages and procedures are based on the program of research and development of Curriculum-Based Measurement of reading by Stan Deno and colleagues at the University of Minnesota (Deno, 1989). There are two components to DORF: oral reading fluency and passage retell. For the oral reading fluency component, students are given an unfamiliar, grade-level passage of text and asked to read for 1 minute. Errors such as substitutions, omissions, and hesitations for more than 3 seconds are marked while listening to the student read aloud. For benchmark assessment, students are asked to read three different grade-level passages for 1 minute each. The score is the median number of words read correctly and the median number of errors across the three passages. Using the median score from three passages gives the best indicator of student performance over a range of different text and content. The oral reading fluency component can be used winter of first grade through spring of sixth grade.

The passage retell component follows the reading of each passage, *provided that the student has read at least 40 words correct per minute on a given passage*. Passage retell is intended to provide a comprehension check for the DORF assessment, and provides an indication that the student is reading for meaning. With a prompted passage retell, the student is instructed to read for meaning. Speed-reading without attending to text comprehension is undesirable and will be readily apparent in the student's retell.

Case studies have documented students who can read words but not comprehend what they read (Dewitz & Dewitz, 2003). There is concern that students who display similar reading behavior will not be identified without a comprehension check. Passage retell provides an efficient procedure to identify those students who are not able to talk about what they have just read. Inclusion of passage retell also explicitly instructs students to be reading fluently for meaning. The quality of a student's retell provides valuable information about overall reading proficiency and oral language skills.

During retell, the student is asked to tell about what he/she has read. Passage retell provides a valuable indicator of reading comprehension. The assessor indicates the number of words in the retell that are related to the passage by drawing through a box of numbers. Following a hesitation of 3 seconds, students are prompted to tell as much as they can about the passage. If the student hesitates again for 5 seconds or longer, or if the student is clearly responding for 5 seconds in a way that is not relevant to the passage, the task is discontinued. The assessor must make a judgment about the relevance of the retell to the passage. Retell can be used from the middle of first grade through the spring of sixth grade. A quality of response rating allows the assessor to make a qualitative rating of the quality of the student's response. The rating should be based on how well the student retold the portion of the passage that he/she read.

Materials

- Scoring Booklet
- Assessment Book
- Pen/pencil
- Clipboard
- Stopwatch

Administration Directions

For Oral Reading Fluency:

Follow these directions exactly each time with each student. Say the words in bold italic type verbatim. Put the student copy of the reading passage in front of the student and say the following:

▶ ***I would like you to read a story to me. Please do your best reading. If you do not know a word, I will read the word for you. Keep reading until I say "stop." Be ready to tell me all about the story when you finish.*** (Place the passage in front of the student.)

▶ **Begin testing.** ***Put your finger under the first word*** (point to the first word of the passage). ***Ready, begin.***

1. Do not read the title to the student. If the student chooses to read the title, do not start the stopwatch until he/she reads the first word of the passage. If the student asks you to tell him/her a word in the title or struggles with a word in the title for 3 seconds, say the word. Do not correct any errors the student makes while reading the title.
2. Start the stopwatch *after* the student says the first word of the passage. If the student is silent or struggles for 3 seconds with the first word of the passage, say the word, mark the word as incorrect, and start the stopwatch.

3. During benchmark assessment, three passages are administered *if the student reads 10 or more words correctly on the first passage*. When administering the second and third passages, use the following shortened directions:

> ***Now read this story to me. Please do your best reading. Ready, begin.***

4. During the testing:

   - Follow along in the student's scoring booklet.
   - Leave blank any words read correctly. Mark a slash (/) through errors (including skipped words).
   - The maximum wait time for each word is three seconds. If the student does not provide the word within 3 seconds, say the word and mark it as incorrect.
   - During benchmark assessment, students read three different passages, for 1 minute each. *If the student reads fewer than 10 words correctly on the first passage*, record his/her score for words correct and errors on the front cover of the booklet, and do not administer passages 2 and 3.
   - At the end of **1 minute**, place a bracket ( ]) in the text after the last word provided by the student. Say ***Stop*** and remove the passage. If the student completes the assessment before 1 minute, stop testing and record the student's score. Scores are not prorated.

   Note: If the student is in the middle of a sentence at the end of 1 minute, you may allow the student to finish the sentence, but score only the words said up to the end of 1 minute.

5. *If the student reads 40 or more words correctly on the passage*, have the student retell what he/she has just read using the directions provided below. *If the student reads fewer than 40 words correctly on a passage*, use professional judgment whether to administer Retell for that passage.

DORF Retell

For Retell:

1. Remove the passage from the student and say the following:

> ***Now tell me as much as you can about the story you just read. Ready, begin.***

2. Start the stopwatch and allow a maximum of 1 minute for the retell.
3. The first time the student stops or hesitates for 3 seconds, select one of the following:

   - If the student has not said anything at all, provides a very limited response, or provides an off-track response, say **Tell me as much as you can about the story.**
   - Otherwise, ask **Can you tell me anything more about the story?** This reminder may be used only once.

   After the reminder, the next time the student hesitates or gets off track for 5 seconds, say ***Thank you***, discontinue the task, and record the score on the front of the student's scoring booklet.

4. During the testing:

   - As the student is responding, move your pen through the Retell numbers grid that appears after the passage to count the number of words the student says that are related to the passage.

- Stop moving your pen through the numbers if the student stops retelling the story or if his/her retell is not relevant to the story just read.
- If the student's response goes on for more than 1 minute, say ***Thank you***, discontinue the task, circle the total number of words in the student's retell, and record the number on the "Retell Total" line.
- When the student has finished responding or has met the discontinue criteria, circle the total number of words in the student's retell, and record the number on the "Retell Total" line.

After Testing:

1. Immediately after testing:
   - Score reading passages immediately after administration. Use the cumulative word count to determine the total number of words read. Record that total on the "Total words" line on the scoring page.
   - Record the number of errors (including skipped words) on the "Errors" line on the scoring page.
   - Subtract the number of errors from the total words to determine the number of words correct and record it on the "Words correct" line.
   - Use the Retell Quality of Response Rubric (below) to rate the quality of the student's retell response, based on the portion of the passage that the student read. These ratings are not used for determining the DORF score, but may be helpful for focusing additional comprehension assessment or comprehension instruction. Circle the retell rating.

     Quality of Response:

1	Provides 2 or fewer details
2	Provides 3 or more details
3	Provides 3 or more details in a meaningful sequence
4	Provides 3 or more details in a meaningful sequence that captures a main idea

2. At a later time (shortly after the testing when you are no longer with the student), compute the student's final DORF scores:
   - During benchmark assessment, if the student reads three passages, record all three "Words correct" scores and all three error counts on the front cover of the student's scoring booklet and circle the median (middle) "Words correct" score and median (middle) error count. For example, if the "Words correct" across the three passages are 42, 28, and 35, circle the 35. If the student's errors are 4, 6, and 7, circle the 6. If two scores are the same number, that number is the median. For example, if the scores are 62, 58, and 62, the median is 62.
   - During benchmark assessment, if the student provides a retell after all three passages, record all three retell scores and all three Quality of Response values on the front cover of the student's scoring booklet and circle the median (middle) score and median (middle) Quality of Response. For example, if the student's retell scores across the three passages are 12, 8, and 5, circle the 8. If two scores are the same number, that number is the median. For example, if the Quality of Response values are 2, 3, and 2, the median is 2. If the student meets the criteria to engage in retell on only two passages, the median is the average of the two numbers.

- Most data management services will calculate the student's accuracy rate for you. To calculate the accuracy yourself, use the following formula:

$$\textit{Accuracy} = 100 \times \frac{\textit{median words correct}}{\textit{median words correct} + \textit{median errors}}$$

Scoring Rules for DORF

The student receives 1 point for each word read correctly in 1 minute.

1. Leave blank any words the student reads correctly. Inserted words are not counted. To be counted as correct, words must be read as whole words and pronounced correctly for the context of the sentence.

2. Mark a slash (/) through any errors. Errors include words read incorrectly, substitutions, skipped words, hesitations of more than 3 seconds, words read out of order, and words that are sounded out but not read as a whole word.

Discontinue Rule

Discontinue administering DORF if the student reads zero words correctly in the first line of the first passage. Record a score of 0 on the "Total words" line on the scoring page and in the DORF "Words correct" score box on the front cover of the student's scoring booklet. If the student reads fewer than 10 words correctly on the first passage during benchmark assessment, do not administer Retell or the second and third passages. If the student reads fewer than 40 words correctly on any passage, use professional judgment on whether to administer Retell for that passage.

Wait Rule

Wait 3 seconds for the student to respond. If the student hesitates for 3 seconds on a word, mark a slash (/) through it and read the word to the student. If necessary, indicate for the student to continue with the next word by pointing.

Reminders

If the student stops reading (and it's not a hesitation on a specific item), say ***Keep going***. *This reminder may be used as often as needed.*

If the student loses her/his place while reading, point. *This reminder may be used as often as needed.*

Note:

Students are not penalized for differences in pronunciation due to dialect, articulation delays or impairments, or for pronunciations due to speaking a first language other than English.

Examples of Scoring Rules

The following are examples of how to score responses on DORF. The examples do not encompass all possible responses. If in doubt about how to score a student response, refer to the scoring rules above. Please pay attention to the notes included with the examples as they provide scoring explanations and indicate variations and nuances related to the scoring.

Correct Response

Scoring Rule 1: **Leave blank any words the student reads correctly. Inserted words are not counted. To be counted as correct, words must be read as whole words and pronounced correctly for the context of the sentence.**

Examples:

Student response It was hot at the beach.

How to score

0	It was hot at the beach.] Mr. Smith doesn't mind the heat. He has	14
14	had a part-time job there as a lifeguard for twenty-four years.	27

Total words: 6

Errors (include skipped words): – 0

Words correct: = 6

Student response It was hot at the /b/ /ea/ /ch/ beach.

How to score

0	It was hot at the beach.] Mr. Smith doesn't mind the heat. He has	14
14	had a part-time job there as a lifeguard for twenty-four years.	27

Total words: 6

Errors (include skipped words): – 0

Words correct: = 6

Note: To be counted as correct, the whole word must be read.

Student response It was hot and sunny at the beach.

How to score

0	It was hot at the beach.] Mr. Smith doesn't mind the heat. He has	14
14	had a part-time job there as a lifeguard for twenty-four years.	27

Total words: 6

Errors (include skipped words): – 0

Words correct: = 6

Note: Inserted words are ignored and not counted as errors. The student does not get additional credit for inserted words. If the student frequently inserts extra words, note the pattern in the Notes section at the bottom of the Retell scoring page.

Student response It was hot at the at the beach.

How to score

0	It was hot at the beach.] Mr. Smith doesn't mind the heat. He has	14
14	had a part-time job there as a lifeguard for twenty-four years.	27

Total words: 6

Errors (include skipped words): – 0

Words correct: = 6

Note: Words that are repeated and phrases that are re-read are not scored as incorrect and are ignored in scoring.

Student response It was hot at the bank…I mean beach.

How to score

0	It was hot at the ~~beach~~ (SC).] Mr. Smith doesn't mind the heat. He has	14
14	had a part-time job there as a lifeguard for twenty-four years.	27

Total words: 6

Errors (include skipped words): – 0

Words correct: = 6

Note: A word is scored as correct if it is initially mispronounced but the student self-corrects within 3 seconds. Mark SC above the word and score as correct.

Student response It was hot at the beach in Dubay.

How to score

0	It was hot at the beach in Dubai.] Mr. Smith doesn't mind the heat.	14
14	He has had a part-time job there as a lifeguard for twenty-four years.	29

Total words: 8

Errors (include skipped words): – 0

Words correct: = 8

Note: If the student reads a proper noun with correct pronunciation or with any reasonable phonetic pronunciation, it is counted as correct. Reasonable phonetic pronunciation includes, but is not limited to, left to right sequential decoding, an accurate number of phonemes, and errors that represent knowledge of probable phonetic decoding based upon English orthography (McGuinness, 1997). This rule applies to all proper nouns.

Correct Response (cont.)

Student response It was hot at the beach. Mister Smith doesn't mind the heat. He has had a part-time job there as a lifeguard for twenty-four years.

How to score

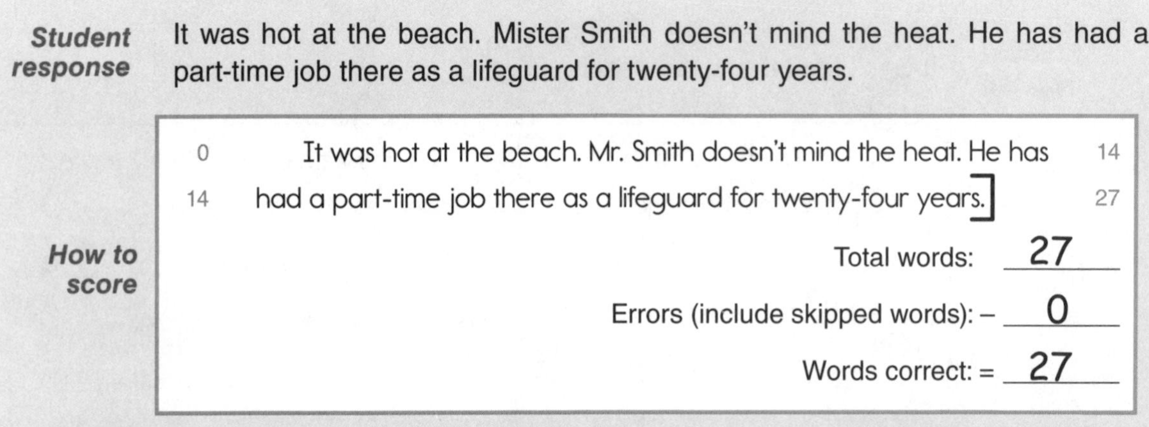

0	It was hot at the beach. Mr. Smith doesn't mind the heat. He has	14
14	had a part-time job there as a lifeguard for twenty-four years.]	27

Total words: 27

Errors (include skipped words): – 0

Words correct: = 27

Note: (1) Abbreviations should be read in the way they would be pronounced in conversation. (2) Numerals must be read correctly within the context of the sentence. (3) Hyphenated words count as two words (and two errors) if both parts can stand alone as individual words. Hyphenated words count as one word if either part cannot stand alone as an individual word (e.g., *x-ray*, *t-shirt*).

Incorrect Response

Scoring Rule 2: **Mark a slash (/) through any errors. Errors include words read incorrectly, substitutions, skipped words, hesitations of more than 3 seconds, words read out of order, and words that are sounded out but not read as a whole word.**

Examples:

Student response It is hot at the beach.

How to score

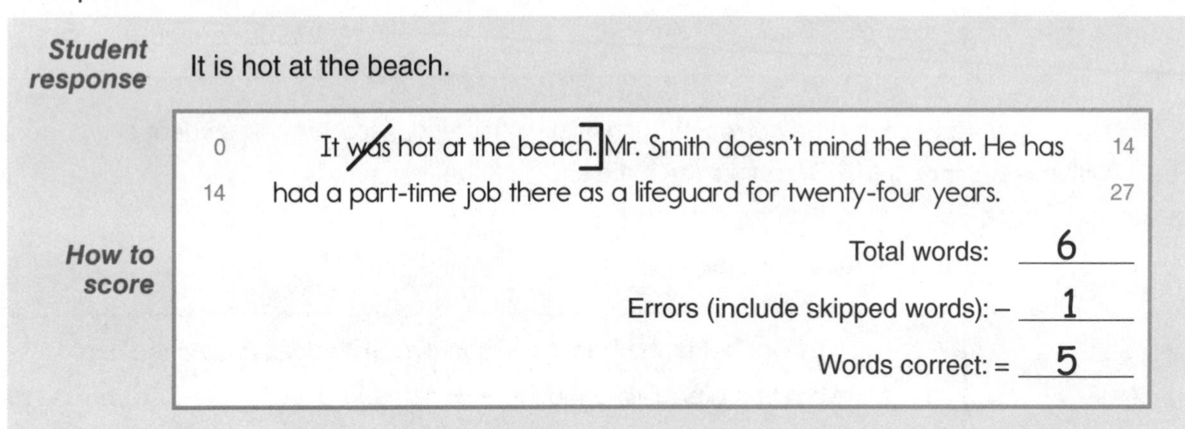

0	It ~~was~~ hot at the beach.] Mr. Smith doesn't mind the heat. He has	14
14	had a part-time job there as a lifeguard for twenty-four years.	27

Total words: 6

Errors (include skipped words): – 1

Words correct: = 5

Student response It was hot at the /b/ /e/ /a/ /ch/.

How to score

0 It was hot at the beach.] Mr. Smith doesn't mind the heat. He has 14
14 had a part-time job there as a lifeguard for twenty-four years. 27

Total words: 6

Errors (include skipped words): – 1

Words correct: = 5

Note: Students must read the whole word, not just the sounds, to be counted as correct.

Student response It was hot at the barn. Mr. Smith doesn't mind the heat. He has had a part-time job at the barn as a lifeguard for twenty-four years.

How to score

0 It was hot at the beach. Mr. Smith doesn't mind the heat. He has 14
14 had a part-time job at the beach as a lifeguard for twenty-four years.] 29

Total words: 29

Errors (include skipped words): – 2

Words correct: = 27

Note: If a student incorrectly reads the same word multiple times in the passage, it counts as an error each time.

Student response It was at the beach.

How to score

0 It was hot at the beach.] Mr. Smith doesn't mind the heat. He has 14
14 had a part-time job there as a lifeguard for twenty-four years. 27

Total words: 6

Errors (include skipped words): – 1

Words correct: = 5

Note: Omitted words are scored as incorrect.

Incorrect Response (cont.)

Student response It was hot at the beach. Mr. Smith doesn't mind the heat. He has usually works on weekends when the beach is crowded.

How to score

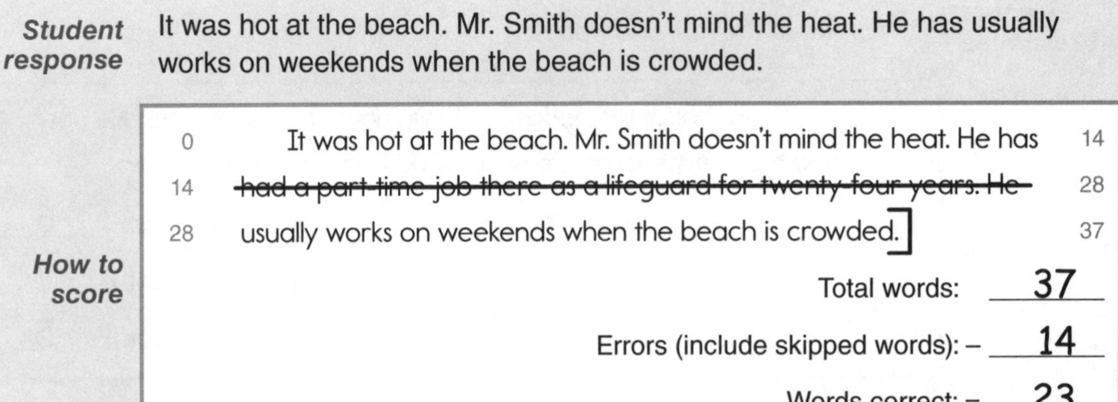

0 It was hot at the beach. Mr. Smith doesn't mind the heat. He has 14
14 ~~had a part-time job there as a lifeguard for twenty-four years. He~~ 28
28 usually works on weekends when the beach is crowded.] 37

Total words: 37
Errors (include skipped words): – 14
Words correct: = 23

Note: If a student skips a row of text, draw a line through the entire row and count the omitted words as errors.

Student response It was high at the beach.

How to score

0 It was ~~hot~~ at the beach.] Mr. Smith doesn't mind the heat. He has 14
14 had a part-time job there as a lifeguard for twenty-four years. 27

Total words: 6
Errors (include skipped words): – 1
Words correct: = 5

Note: If a student substitutes a word for the word that is written on the page, it is an error.

Student response It was hot at the b…b…b…be...(3 seconds)...(assessor says "beach").

How to score

0 It was hot at the ~~beach~~.] Mr. Smith doesn't mind the heat. He has 14
14 had a part-time job there as a lifeguard for twenty-four years. 27

Total words: 6
Errors (include skipped words): – 1
Words correct: = 5

Note: If a student hesitates or struggles with a word for 3 seconds, tell the student the word and mark the word as incorrect. If necessary, indicate for the student to continue with the next word by pointing.

Student response Mr. Smith duv into the ocean to cool off.

How to score

0	Mr. Smith ~~dove~~ into the ocean to cool off.] It was hot at the	14
14	beach but Mr. Smith didn't mind. He has had a part-time job there	28
28	as a lifeguard for twenty-four years.	35

Total words: 9

Errors (include skipped words): – 1

Words correct: = 8

Note: If a word is pronounced incorrectly given the context of the sentence, it is scored as an error.

Student response It was hot at the beach. Mister Smith does not mind the heat. He has had a part-time job there as a lifeguard for twenty-four years.

How to score

0	It was hot at the beach. Mr. Smith ~~doesn't~~ mind the heat. He has	14
14	had a part-time job there as a lifeguard for twenty-four years.]	27

Total words: 27

Errors (include skipped words): – 1

Words correct: = 26

Note: Students should read contractions as they are printed on the page.

Student response It was hot at the beach. Mister Smith doesn't heat the mind. He has had a part-time job there as a lifeguard for twenty-four years.

How to score

0	It was hot at the beach. Mr. Smith doesn't ~~mind~~ the ~~heat~~. He has	14
14	had a part-time job there as a lifeguard for twenty-four years.]	27

Total words: 27

Errors (include skipped words): – 2

Words correct: = 25

Note: Words must be read in the order they appear on the page to be considered a correctly read word.

Scoring Rules for Retell

Scoring Rules for Retell

The student receives 1 point for every word in his/her retell that is related to the passage.

1. Count as correct any words in the response that are related to the passage. The judgment is based on whether the student is retelling the passage or has gotten off track on another passage or topic. Move your pen through a number in the scoring booklet for each word the student provides that is related to the passage.

2. Count as incorrect any words in the response that are not related to the passage the student is reading. Do not move your pen through a number in the scoring booklet for words that are not related to the passage the student is reading.

Discontinue Rule

Discontinue Rule

After the first Wait Rule reminder (see below), if the student does not say anything or gets off track for 5 seconds, say ***Thank you*** and discontinue the task.

Wait Rule

Wait Rule/Reminder

If the student stops or hesitates for 3 seconds, select one of the following:

- If the student has not said anything at all, provides a very limited response, or provides an off-track response, say ***Tell me as much as you can about the story.***
- Otherwise, ask ***Can you tell me anything more about the story?*** This reminder may be used only once.

Note:

The student is not penalized for language use or grammatical errors that are due to articulation, dialect, or speaking a first language other than English.

Examples of Scoring Rules

The following are examples of the Retell scoring rules. The examples do not encompass all possible responses. If in doubt about how to score a student response, refer to the scoring rules above. Please pay attention to the notes included with the examples of responses as they provide scoring explanations and indicate variations and nuances related to the scoring.

Correct Response

Scoring Rule 1: Count as correct any words in the response that are related to the passage. The judgment is based on whether the student is retelling the passage or has gotten off track on another passage or topic. Move your pen through a number in the scoring booklet for each word the student provides that is related to the passage.

Examples:

Passage Goldfish make good pets. They are easy to take care of and do not cost much to feed. Goldfish are fun to watch while they are swimming.

Student response He has a pet goldfish. The fish is easy to take care of. He likes to watch it swim. It is a good pet.

How to score

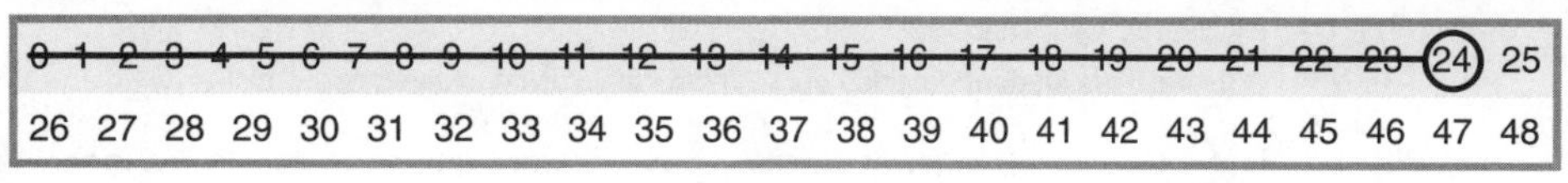

Retell Total: 24

Quality of Response:
(Note: If the student provides only a main idea, it is considered one detail.)

1 Provides 2 or fewer details
2 Provides 3 or more details
3 Provides 3 or more details in a meaningful sequence
(4) Provides 3 or more details in a meaningful sequence that captures a main idea

Student response He's got a pet goldfish because goldfish make good pets. He takes good care of his fish. He likes to watch it swim.

How to score

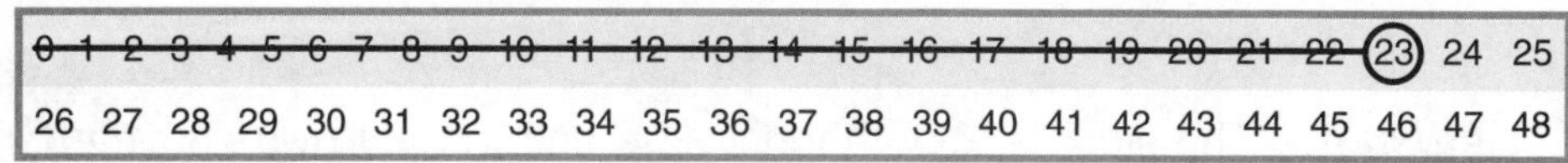

Retell Total: 23

Quality of Response:
(Note: If the student provides only a main idea, it is considered one detail.)

1 Provides 2 or fewer details
2 Provides 3 or more details
3 Provides 3 or more details in a meaningful sequence
(4) Provides 3 or more details in a meaningful sequence that captures a main idea

Note: Contractions are counted as one word.

Student response The story is about a girl who has a goldfish and she really likes it.

How to score

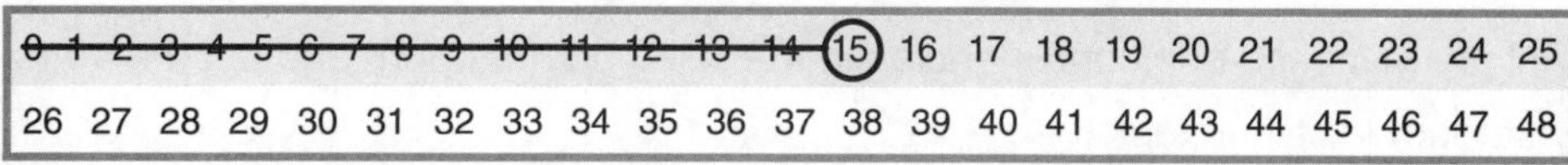

Retell Total: 15

Quality of Response:
(Note: If the student provides only a main idea, it is considered one detail.)

1 Provides 2 or fewer details
2 Provides 3 or more details
(3) Provides 3 or more details in a meaningful sequence
4 Provides 3 or more details in a meaningful sequence that captures a main idea

Correct Response (cont.)

Student response Goldfish. And pets.

How to score

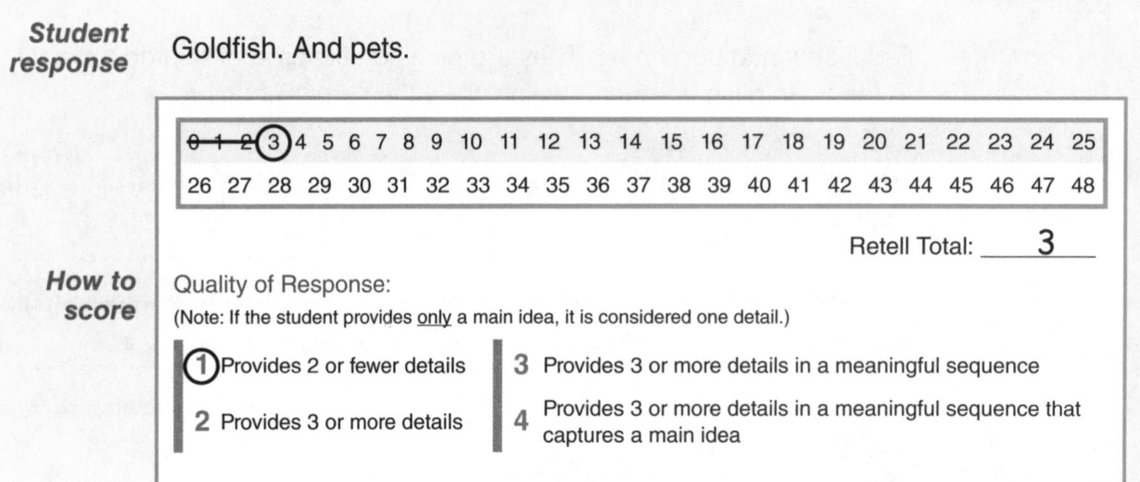

~~0~~	~~1~~	~~2~~	(3)	4	5	6	7	8	9	10	11	12	13	14	15	16	17	18	19	20	21	22	23	24	25
26	27	28	29	30	31	32	33	34	35	36	37	38	39	40	41	42	43	44	45	46	47	48			

Retell Total: 3

Quality of Response:
(Note: If the student provides only a main idea, it is considered one detail.)

(1) Provides 2 or fewer details
2 Provides 3 or more details
3 Provides 3 or more details in a meaningful sequence
4 Provides 3 or more details in a meaningful sequence that captures a main idea

Passage During the last ice age, the world looked much different than it does today. Nearly all the land was covered with huge sheets of ice or glaciers. Most of the world's water was trapped in these glaciers, and the water level of the seas was low. A vast amount of land was above the water.

The narrow waterway between Asia and North America, the Bering Strait, was mostly exposed land at that time. The land formed a narrow bridge that connected Asia with North America.

Student response The story is about the ice age and the land was covered in ice. There were glaciers. And there was a land bridge between Asia and South America.

How to score

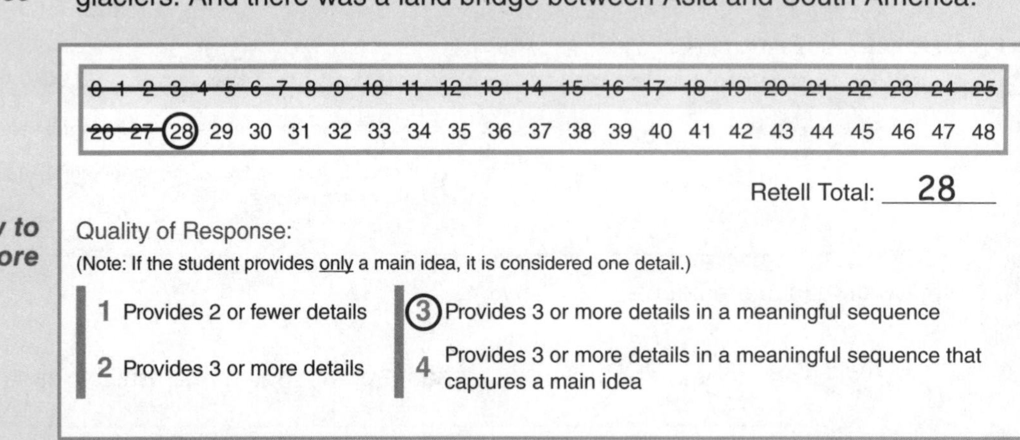

~~0~~	~~1~~	~~2~~	~~3~~	~~4~~	~~5~~	~~6~~	~~7~~	~~8~~	~~9~~	~~10~~	~~11~~	~~12~~	~~13~~	~~14~~	~~15~~	~~16~~	~~17~~	~~18~~	~~19~~	~~20~~	~~21~~	~~22~~	~~23~~	~~24~~	~~25~~
~~26~~	~~27~~	(28)	29	30	31	32	33	34	35	36	37	38	39	40	41	42	43	44	45	46	47	48			

Retell Total: 28

Quality of Response:
(Note: If the student provides only a main idea, it is considered one detail.)

1 Provides 2 or fewer details
2 Provides 3 or more details
(3) Provides 3 or more details in a meaningful sequence
4 Provides 3 or more details in a meaningful sequence that captures a main idea

Note: Mistakes or inconsistencies in the retell do not count against the student as long as the student is still on topic.

Passage

The main ingredients for this recipe are cucumbers and dill weed. Both of these are easy to grow if you are lucky enough to have a vegetable garden. If you don't have a garden, you can find them in the produce department at the grocery store. Two other produce items you will need are fresh garlic and a small onion about the size of a golf ball. You will also need salt and sugar to add flavor to the pickles.

Student response

It was about making dill pickles. Pickles are made from cucumbers and dill weed. You can grow those in your garden or buy them at the store. You need salt, sugar, some garlic, and an onion the size of a baseball.

How to score

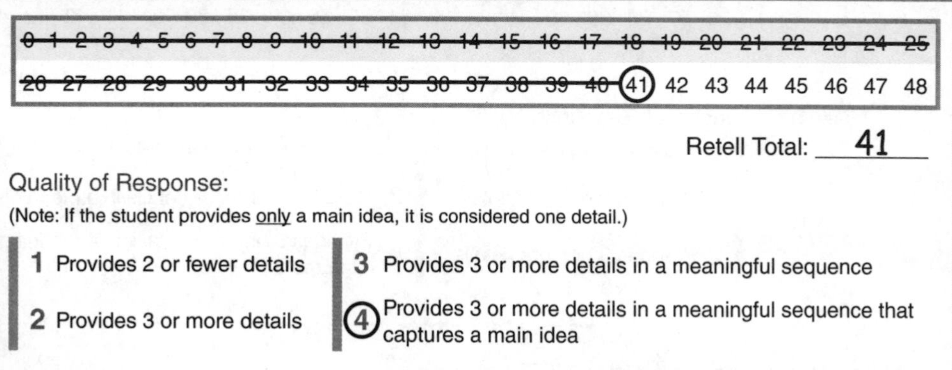

~~0 1 2 3 4 5 6 7 8 9 10 11 12 13 14 15 16 17 18 19 20 21 22 23 24 25~~

~~26 27 28 29 30 31 32 33 34 35 36 37 38 39 40~~ (41) 42 43 44 45 46 47 48

Retell Total: 41

Quality of Response:

(Note: If the student provides only a main idea, it is considered one detail.)

1 Provides 2 or fewer details

2 Provides 3 or more details

3 Provides 3 or more details in a meaningful sequence

(4) Provides 3 or more details in a meaningful sequence that captures a main idea

Note: Mistakes or inconsistencies in the retell do not count against the student as long as the student is still on topic.

Incorrect Response

Scoring Rule 2: **Stop moving your pen through the numbers and count as incorrect any response that is not related to the story that the student read.**

Examples:

Passage Goldfish make good pets. They are easy to take care of and do not cost much to feed. Goldfish are fun to watch while they are swimming.

Student response He has a pet goldfish. He likes to watch it swim. **I like to swim. We go swimming every Saturday.**

How to score

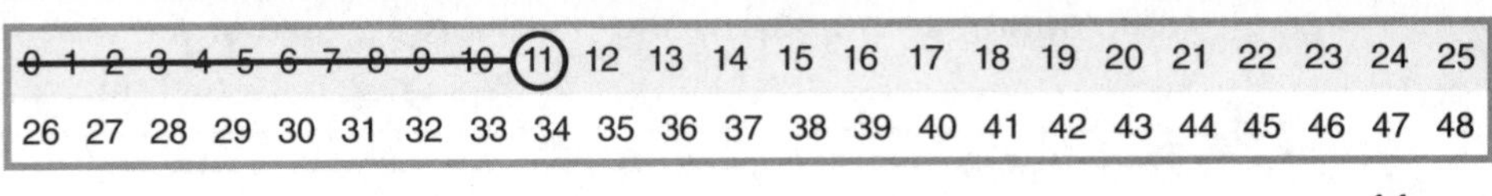

Retell Total: 11

Quality of Response:
(Note: If the student provides only a main idea, it is considered one detail.)

(1) Provides 2 or fewer details	3 Provides 3 or more details in a meaningful sequence
2 Provides 3 or more details	4 Provides 3 or more details in a meaningful sequence that captures a main idea

Note: The portion in bold is NOT counted.

Student response He has a **uhh, a uhh** pet goldfish. The **uhh** fish is easy to **uhh** take care of, **uhh** he likes to **uhh** watch it **uhh** swim.

How to score

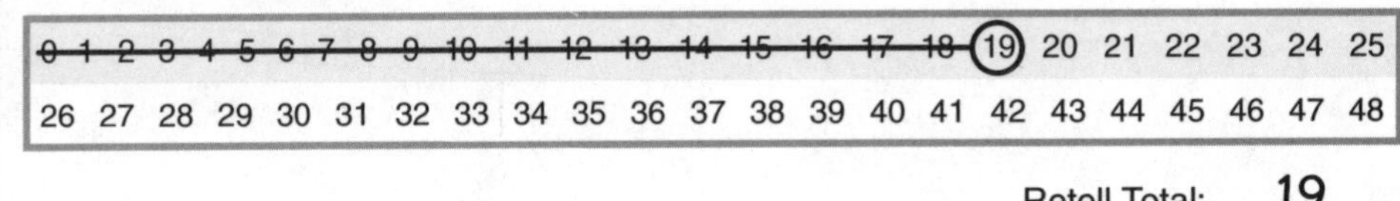

Retell Total: 19

Quality of Response:
(Note: If the student provides only a main idea, it is considered one detail.)

1 Provides 2 or fewer details	(3) Provides 3 or more details in a meaningful sequence
2 Provides 3 or more details	4 Provides 3 or more details in a meaningful sequence that captures a main idea

Student response

He has a pet goldfish. The fish is easy to take care of. He likes to watch it swim. **Mmmm. Hmmm,** it sure is a good pet.

How to score

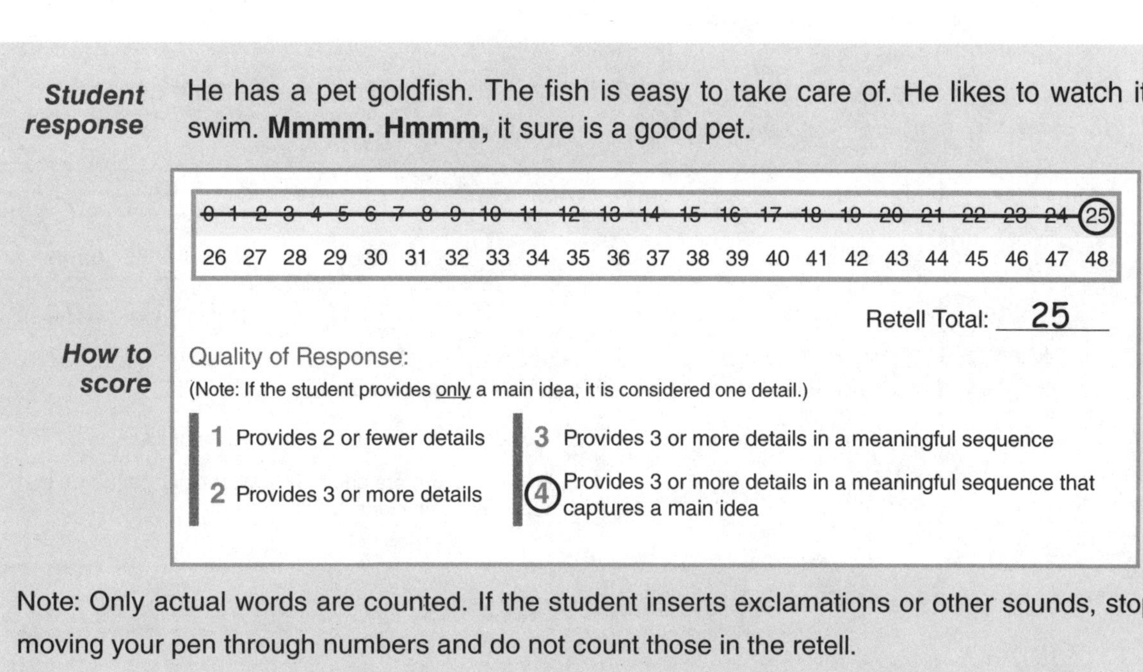

~~0 1 2 3 4 5 6 7 8 9 10 11 12 13 14 15 16 17 18 19 20 21 22 23 24~~ (25)
26 27 28 29 30 31 32 33 34 35 36 37 38 39 40 41 42 43 44 45 46 47 48

Retell Total: 25

Quality of Response:
(Note: If the student provides only a main idea, it is considered one detail.)

1 Provides 2 or fewer details
2 Provides 3 or more details
3 Provides 3 or more details in a meaningful sequence
(4) Provides 3 or more details in a meaningful sequence that captures a main idea

Note: Only actual words are counted. If the student inserts exclamations or other sounds, stop moving your pen through numbers and do not count those in the retell.

Student response

He has a pet goldfish. **I know what rhymes with fish–wish and dish!**

How to score

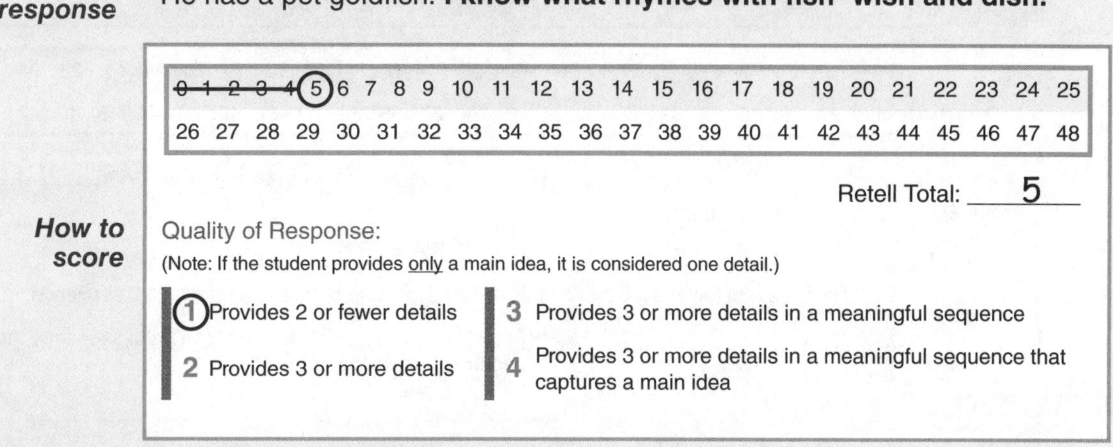

~~0 1 2 3 4~~ (5) 6 7 8 9 10 11 12 13 14 15 16 17 18 19 20 21 22 23 24 25
26 27 28 29 30 31 32 33 34 35 36 37 38 39 40 41 42 43 44 45 46 47 48

Retell Total: 5

Quality of Response:
(Note: If the student provides only a main idea, it is considered one detail.)

(1) Provides 2 or fewer details
2 Provides 3 or more details
3 Provides 3 or more details in a meaningful sequence
4 Provides 3 or more details in a meaningful sequence that captures a main idea

Note: If the student recites the ABC's, a poem, or sings a song, even if relevant to the retell, the recitation, song, or poem is not counted.

Student response He has a pet goldfish **fish fishy fish**. The fish is easy to take care of. He likes to watch it **swimmy** swim **swim**. It is a good pet.

How to score

~~0 1 2 3 4 5 6 7 8 9 10 11 12 13 14 15 16 17 18 19 20 21 22 23~~ (24) 25
26 27 28 29 30 31 32 33 34 35 36 37 38 39 40 41 42 43 44 45 46 47 48

Retell Total: 24

Quality of Response:
(Note: If the student provides only a main idea, it is considered one detail.)

- 1 Provides 2 or fewer details
- 2 Provides 3 or more details
- (3) Provides 3 or more details in a meaningful sequence
- 4 Provides 3 or more details in a meaningful sequence that captures a main idea

Note: Repetitions of words or phrases are not counted.

Student response Goldfish make good pets. **Goldfish make good pets** because they are easy to care for and are cheap to buy.

How to score

~~0 1 2 3 4 5 6 7 8 9 10 11 12 13 14 15~~ (16) 17 18 19 20 21 22 23 24 25
26 27 28 29 30 31 32 33 34 35 36 37 38 39 40 41 42 43 44 45 46 47 48

Retell Total: 16

Quality of Response:
(Note: If the student provides only a main idea, it is considered one detail.)

- 1 Provides 2 or fewer details
- 2 Provides 3 or more details
- 3 Provides 3 or more details in a meaningful sequence
- (4) Provides 3 or more details in a meaningful sequence that captures a main idea

Note: Repetitions of words or phrases are not counted.

Student response **I wish I had a goldfish.**

How to score

(0) 1 2 3 4 5 6 7 8 9 10 11 12 13 14 15 16 17 18 19 20 21 22 23 24 25
26 27 28 29 30 31 32 33 34 35 36 37 38 39 40 41 42 43 44 45 46 47 48

Retell Total: 0

Quality of Response:
(Note: If the student provides only a main idea, it is considered one detail.)

- (1) Provides 2 or fewer details
- 2 Provides 3 or more details
- 3 Provides 3 or more details in a meaningful sequence
- 4 Provides 3 or more details in a meaningful sequence that captures a main idea

Note: The student's entire response is off-track.

Student response

The story is about goldfish as pets. They make good ones because they are easy to care for and are cheap to buy. **I wish I had a goldfish.**

How to score

~~0 1 2 3 4 5 6 7 8 9 10 11 12 13 14 15 16 17 18 19 20 21 22~~ (23) 24 25
26 27 28 29 30 31 32 33 34 35 36 37 38 39 40 41 42 43 44 45 46 47 48

Retell Total: 23

Quality of Response:
(Note: If the student provides only a main idea, it is considered one detail.)

- 1 Provides 2 or fewer details
- 2 Provides 3 or more details
- 3 Provides 3 or more details in a meaningful sequence
- (4) Provides 3 or more details in a meaningful sequence that captures a main idea

Student response

I have to feed our pet dog. I hate to do that job because it is smelly and messy. I wish my mom would just do it.

How to score

(0) 1 2 3 4 5 6 7 8 9 10 11 12 13 14 15 16 17 18 19 20 21 22 23 24 25
26 27 28 29 30 31 32 33 34 35 36 37 38 39 40 41 42 43 44 45 46 47 48

Retell Total: 0

Quality of Response:
(Note: If the student provides only a main idea, it is considered one detail.)

- (1) Provides 2 or fewer details
- 2 Provides 3 or more details
- 3 Provides 3 or more details in a meaningful sequence
- 4 Provides 3 or more details in a meaningful sequence that captures a main idea

Student response

Goldfish make good pets...(pause). **You know, I don't have a goldfish, but I wish I did. I have to feed our pet dog. I hate to do that job because it is smelly and messy. I wish my mom would just do it.**

How to score

~~0 1 2 3~~ (4) 5 6 7 8 9 10 11 12 13 14 15 16 17 18 19 20 21 22 23 24 25
26 27 28 29 30 31 32 33 34 35 36 37 38 39 40 41 42 43 44 45 46 47 48

Retell Total: 4

Quality of Response:
(Note: If the student provides only a main idea, it is considered one detail.)

- (1) Provides 2 or fewer details
- 2 Provides 3 or more details
- 3 Provides 3 or more details in a meaningful sequence
- 4 Provides 3 or more details in a meaningful sequence that captures a main idea

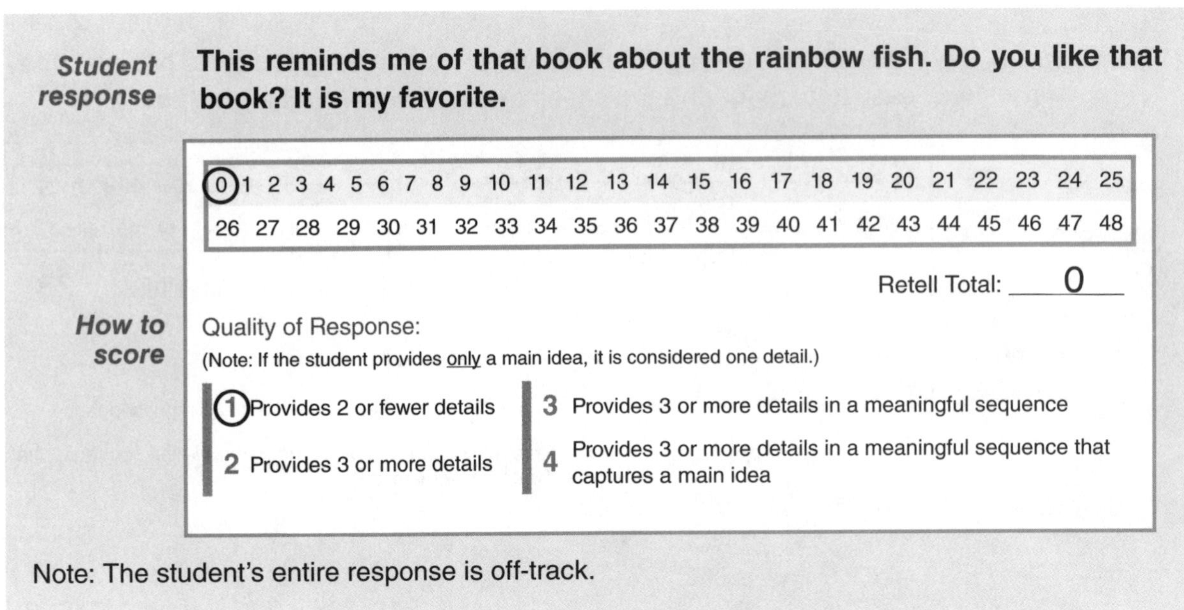

Student response **This reminds me of that book about the rainbow fish. Do you like that book? It is my favorite.**

(0) 1 2 3 4 5 6 7 8 9 10 11 12 13 14 15 16 17 18 19 20 21 22 23 24 25
26 27 28 29 30 31 32 33 34 35 36 37 38 39 40 41 42 43 44 45 46 47 48

Retell Total: 0

How to score Quality of Response:
(Note: If the student provides only a main idea, it is considered one detail.)

(1) Provides 2 or fewer details
2 Provides 3 or more details
3 Provides 3 or more details in a meaningful sequence
4 Provides 3 or more details in a meaningful sequence that captures a main idea

Note: The student's entire response is off-track.

See Appendix 2, pages 123 and 124, for Practice Scoring Sheet and Answer Key.

Model DORF Scoring Sheet

The following is an example of a completed scoring sheet. The scoring rules and scoring calculation are shown. This scoring sheet serves as a model and can be used during training and practice to support accurate administration and scoring of DIBELS.

16 DIBELS® Oral Reading Fluency

Kinds of Hats

0 A hat sits on top of the head. There are many kinds of hats. Some 15
15 hats have special jobs, and some hats are just for fun. 26
26 A hard hat keeps the head safe. It is made out of plastic. House 40
40 ~~builders wear this kind of hat. Things that fall cannot hurt their heads.~~ 53
53 Firefighters also use a hard hat. Their hats have a wide brim on the back 68
68 to keep fire and heat away. You also wear a hard hat when you ride a 84
84 bike. That hat is called a helmet. 91
91 Many workers wear hats that show the job they do. Some of these 104
104 hats are made of cloth. Police officers wear a flat hat that is the same 119
119 color as their uniform. Chefs wear tall white hats when they cook. 131
131 People use different hats to match the weather. Wool hats fit closely 143
143 over the head. They keep the head and ears warm in the winter. Sun 157
157 hats and baseball caps have a wide brim or bill. These hats shade the 171
171 face and eyes from the sun in the summer. 180
180 Hats don't always have a job. Some are just for fun. Birthday party 193
193 hats are made of paper. They have bright colors and cute pictures. 205
205 Next time you walk in the neighborhood, go on a hat hunt. You will 219
219 be surprised at how many different hats you can find. 229

Total words: 73

Errors (include skipped words): – 15

Words correct: = 58

Basic Early Literacy Skill	*DIBELS* Indicator
Reading Comprehension	Daze

What is reading comprehension?

Early reading acquisition is a large, complex linguistic task, whereby students gain knowledge about speech sounds, print rules, and strategies for decoding words. Reading comprehension is equally large and complex, and is best understood as an interactive process between the reader's skills and context. Reading comprehension is the ability to understand what is read, and is demonstrated by making inferences, getting the gist, filling in the gaps, and understanding the big ideas of the text (Duke, Pressley, & Hilden, 2004).

While reading comprehension is dependent on decoding skills, decoding skills by themselves are not enough (Adams, 1990). In order to understand the printed words, readers must tap into their knowledge about language as well as their understanding of the world. Reading comprehension thus requires accurate, effortless decoding (Adams, 1990); access to linguistic knowledge about syntax, semantics, and word morphology (Catts & Kahmi, 1999; McGuinness, 2005); prior knowledge about words in a given context (Duke, Pressley & Hilden, 2004); and reasoning skills. It is only through the skillful interplay of both bottom-up decoding skills and top-down meaning-making skills that the student reads, and reads for meaning.

Students' ability to read and understand increasingly difficult texts increases as they develop more sophisticated decoding skills, improve their vocabulary knowledge and linguistic awareness, and gain experience with the world. Effective reading comprehension instruction that supports the acquisition of comprehension strategies applied to a wide range of reading materials is essential.

Chapter 10: **Daze**

Overview

Basic Early Literacy Skill	Reading Comprehension
Administration Time	3 minutes
Administration Schedule	Beginning of third grade to end of sixth grade
Score	Number of correct words in 3 minutes minus half the number of incorrect words

What is Daze?

Daze is a new measure in *DIBELS Next*. Daze is the standardized *DIBELS* version of maze procedures for measuring reading comprehension. The purpose of a maze procedure is to measure the reasoning processes that constitute comprehension. Specifically, Daze assesses the student's ability to construct meaning from text using word recognition skills, background information and prior knowledge, familiarity with linguistic properties such as syntax and morphology, and reasoning skills.

Daze can be given to a whole class at the same time, to a small group of students, or to individual students. Using standardized directions, students are asked to read a passage silently and to circle their word choices. By design, approximately every seventh word in the Daze passages has been replaced by a box containing the correct word and two distractor words. The student receives credit for selecting the words that best fit the omitted words in the reading passage. The scores that are recorded are the number of correct and incorrect responses. An adjusted score, which compensates for guessing, is calculated based on the number of correct and incorrect responses.

Materials

- Student Booklet
- Pen/pencil
- Daze Benchmark Assessment Administration Directions and Scoring Keys
- Clipboard and stopwatch

Administration Directions

Follow these directions exactly each time with each student. Say the words in bold italic type verbatim. Begin with the modeling and practice activities. The practice activities are designed to introduce the assessment task to the student. They are untimed and include correction procedures. The correction procedures are not used once the timing begins.

1. Before handing out the worksheets, say ***I am going to give you a worksheet. When you get your worksheet, please write your name at the top and put your pencil down.*** Hand out the Daze student worksheets. Make sure each student has the appropriate worksheet. If the worksheets are in a booklet, make sure each student's booklet is open to the correct worksheet.

   When all of the students are ready, say ***You are going to read a story with some missing words. For each missing word there will be a box with three words. Circle the word that makes the most sense in the story. Look at Practice 1.***

   Listen. After playing in the dirt, Sam went (pause) ***home, summer, was*** (pause) ***to wash her hands. You should circle the word "home" because "home" makes the most sense in the story. Listen. After playing in the dirt, Sam went <u>home</u> to wash her hands.***

   Now it is your turn. Read Practice 2 <u>silently</u>. When you come to a box, read all the words in the box and circle the word that makes the most sense in the story. When you are done, put your pencil down.

   Allow up to 30 seconds for students to complete the example and put their pencils down. If necessary, after 30 seconds say ***Put your pencil down.***

2. As soon as all students have their pencils down, say ***Listen. On her way home, she*** (pause) ***chair, sleep, saw*** (pause) ***an ice cream truck. You should have circled "saw" because "saw" makes the most sense in the story. Listen. On her way home, she <u>saw</u> an ice cream truck.***

   When I say "begin," turn the page over and start reading the story silently. When you come to a box, read all the words in the box and circle the word that makes the most sense in the story. Ready? Begin. Start your stopwatch after you say "begin."

3. Monitor students to ensure they are reading and circling the words. Use the reminders as needed.

4. At the end of **3 minutes**, stop your stopwatch and say ***Stop. Put your pencil down.*** Collect all of the Daze worksheet packets.

At a later time (shortly after the testing when you are no longer with the student), compute the final score:

- Correct the worksheets and calculate each student's number of correct and incorrect responses. If a student completes the assessment before the time is up, do not prorate the score.
- Record both scores on the cover sheet. On the cover sheet, "C" designates correct responses and "I" designates incorrect responses. For benchmark assessment, also transfer the score to the front of the scoring booklet. For progress monitoring, there is no scoring booklet for Daze, but there is a progress monitoring chart to record the scores.

- The Daze Adjusted Score is a modified score that compensates for student guessing. Most data management services will calculate the Adjusted Score for you. To calculate the Adjusted Score yourself, use the following formula:

  Daze Adjusted Score = number of correct responses – (number of incorrect responses ÷ 2).

  The result of the formula should be rounded to the nearest whole number. Half-points (0.5) should be rounded up. The minimum Daze Adjusted Score is 0. Do not record a negative number.

Scoring Rules

The student receives 1 point for each correct word, minus half a point for each incorrect word.

1. A response is correct if the student circled or otherwise marked the correct word.
2. Mark a slash (/) through any incorrect responses. Incorrect responses include errors, boxes with more than one answer marked, and items left blank (if they occur before the last item the student attempted within the 3-minute time limit). Items left blank because the student could not get to them before time ran out do not need to be slashed and do not count as incorrect responses.
3. If there are erasure marks, scratched out words, or any other extraneous markings, and the student's final response is obvious, score the item based on that response.

Discontinue Rule

There is no discontinue rule.

Wait Rule

There is no wait rule.

Reminders

If a student starts reading the passage aloud, say **Remember to read the story silently**. *This reminder may be used as often as needed.*

If a student is not working on the task, say **Remember to circle the word in each box that makes the most sense in the story.** *This reminder may be used as often as needed.*

If a student asks you to provide a word for him/her, or for general help with the task, say **Just do your best**. *This reminder may be used as often as needed.*

Examples of Scoring Rules

The following are examples of how to score Daze responses. The examples do not encompass all possible responses. If in doubt about how to score a student response, refer to the scoring rules on the previous page. Please pay attention to the notes included with the examples as they provide scoring explanations and indicate variations and nuances related to the scoring.

Correct Response

Scoring Rule 1: A response is correct if the student circled or otherwise marked the correct word.

Example:

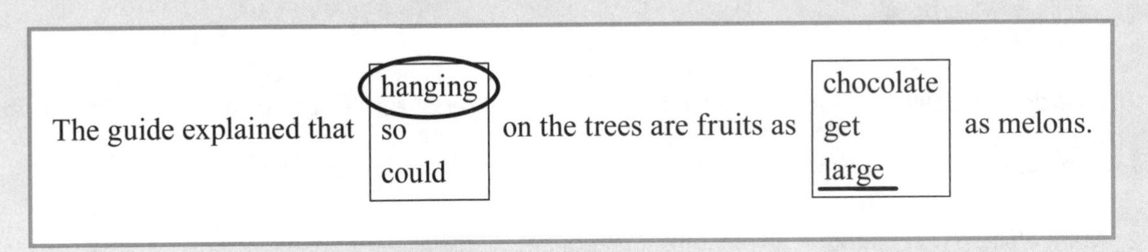

Incorrect Response

Scoring Rule 2: Mark a slash (/) through any incorrect responses. Incorrect responses include errors, boxes with more than one answer marked, and items left blank (if they occur before the last item the student attempted within the 3-minute time limit). Items left blank because the student could not get to them before time ran out do not need to be slashed and do not count as incorrect responses.

Example:

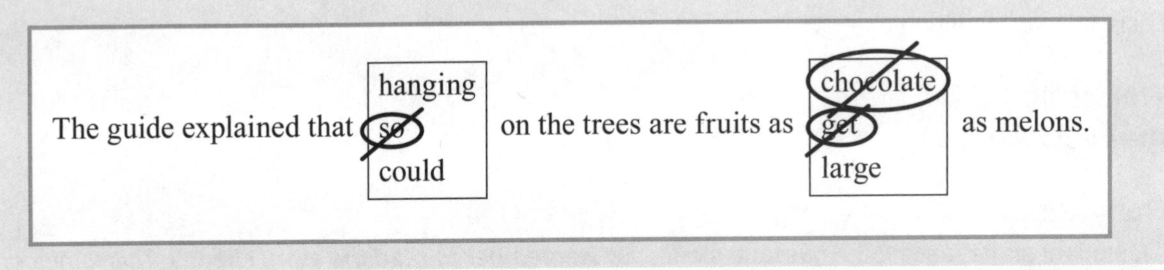

Erasure Marks

Scoring Rule 3: If there are erasure marks, scratched-out words, or any other extraneous markings, and the student's final response is obvious, score the item based on that response.

Example:

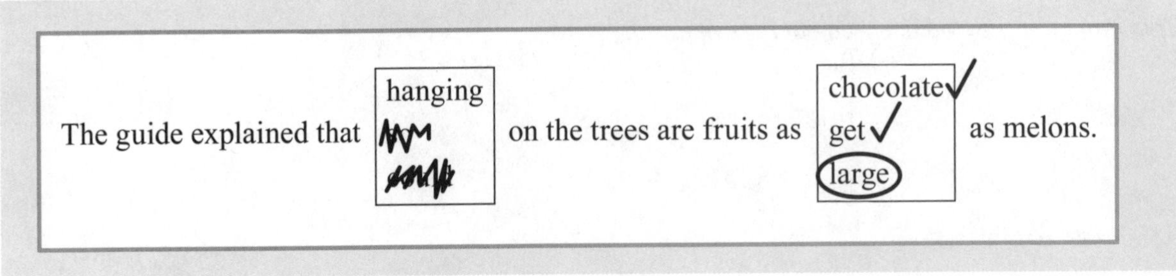

Appendices

Appendix 1: **Pronunciation Guide** 115

Appendix 2: **Practice Scoring Sheets and Answer Keys** 117

Appendix 3: **Assessment Accuracy Checklists** 125

Appendix 4: **Sample Statement and Letters** 133

Appendix 5: **Benchmark Goals and Cut Points for Risk** 137

Appendix 6: ***DIBELS* Composite Score** 147

Appendix 1: Pronunciation Guide

The Pronunciation Guide is a reference for giving and scoring the *DIBELS* measures. The phonemes and examples should guide how the sounds are spoken to students during the assessment, and also should guide how to score the measures. The sounds listed in this guide are shown in the initial, medial, and final position in words when possible. Multiple spellings (or the most common spellings) for each sound are shown. Different regions of the country use different dialects of American English. Any regional or dialectal pronunciation of the sound is acceptable.

Phoneme	Phoneme Example	Phoneme	Phoneme Example
/b/	**b**us, **b**a**b**y, tu**b**	/TH/	**th**em, fea**th**er, brea**the**
/d/	**d**ig, **d**oll, la**dd**er, hi**d**	/ng/	wi**ng**, spinni**ng**, thi**n**k, ru**ng**
/f/	**f**ox, be**f**ore, lau**gh,** gra**ph**	/a/	**a**nt, t**a**p, h**a**t
/g/	**g**o, le**g**, so**gg**y, ho**g**	/e/	**e**cho, h**e**n, m**e**t
/h/	**h**im, a**h**ead	/i/	**i**s, s**i**t, b**i**g, w**i**th
/j/	**j**ar, le**dg**e, **j**ump, a**g**ile	/o/	**o**ff, s**aw**, d**o**t, w**a**ffle
/k/	**c**ap, **k**ite, ba**k**ing, e**ch**o, sta**ck**	/u/	**u**p, **a**llow, ab**o**ve, m**o**ther
/l/	**l**ap, **l**ight, ho**ll**ow, pu**ll**	/ai/	**a**ce, r**ai**l, m**a**de, h**ay**
/m/	**m**ess, **m**e, ha**mm**er, su**m,** a**m**	/ea/	**ea**t, fl**ee**t, sh**e**
/n/	**n**ot, di**nn**er, o**n**	/ie/	**i**ce, tr**ie**d, f**i**nally, p**ie, igh**t, fl**y**
/p/	**p**ie, a**pp**le, ho**p**	/oa/	**oa**k, s**oa**p, h**o**pe
/r/	**r**un, t**r**ee, **wr**ite, a**rr**ow	/oo/	b**oo**t, sh**oe**, val**ue**, neph**ew**
/s/	**s**ap, **c**ity, li**s**ten, ra**c**e	/uu/	w**oo**d, sh**ou**ld, p**u**t
/t/	**t**ot, ho**tt**er, ma**t**	/ow/	h**ou**se, c**ow**
/v/	**v**est, **v**ase, se**v**en, mo**v**e	/oy/	**oi**l, p**oi**nt, ch**oi**ce, t**oy**
/w/	**w**in, a**w**ay, **wh**eel, some**wh**ere	/ar/ (1 phoneme)	**ar**t, h**ear**t, st**ar**t
/y/	**y**es, on**i**on	/er/ (1 phoneme)	f**er**n, f**ir**st, l**ear**n, t**ur**n, g**ir**l
/z/	**z**ip, ea**s**y, i**s**	/or/ (1 phoneme)	s**or**t, bef**ore**
/ch/	**ch**icken, fu**t**ure, swi**tch**	/e/ /r/ (2 phonemes)	p**air**, sh**are**
/sh/	**sh**op, **sh**ow, mo**ti**on, hu**sh**	/i/ /r/ (2 phonemes)	h**ear**
/zh/	trea**s**ure, bei**ge**	/uu/ /r/ (2 phonemes)	t**our**, l**ure**
/th/	**th**ink, no**th**ing, sou**th**		

Note: For the intent and purpose of assessing beginning phonemic awareness skills in students in kindergarten and first grade, we do not distinguish between the /w/ sound in "win" and the /wh/ sound in "where" or between the /o/ sound in "hop" and the /aw/ sound in "saw."

Appendix 2: Practice Scoring Sheets and Answer Keys

The following tables provide an opportunity for self-directed practice in scoring student responses. This practice is intended to supplement and not replace training on the administration and scoring of the measures.

First Sound Fluency Practice Scoring Sheet

Word	Student Response	Score	Rule/Note
ramp	r		
	ra		
	ram		
	ramp		
fast	f		
	fa		
	fas		
	fast		
slip	s		
	sl		
	sli		
	slip		
breeze	f		
	fr		
	frea		
	breaz		
plate	pu		
	plu		
	plai		
	plait		
trade	ch*		
	chai		
	chaid		

*said by a student with speech impairment; pronounces /ch/ for /tr/ and /j/ for /dr/

First Sound Fluency Practice Scoring Sheet: Answer Key

Word	Student Response	Score	Rule/Note
ramp	r	2	Correct first sound
	ra	1	Blended first sounds
	ram	0	Included sounds beyond the first vowel
	ramp	0	Repeat word
fast	f	2	Correct first sound
	fa	1	Blended first sounds
	fas	0	Included sounds beyond the first vowel
	fast	0	Repeat word
slip	s	2	Correct first sound
	sl	1	Blended first sounds
	sli	1	Blended first sounds
	slip	0	Repeat word
breeze	f	0	Incorrect first sound
	fr	0	Incorrect blended first sound
	frea	0	Incorrect blended first sound
	breaz	0	Repeat word
plate	pu	2	Correct with added sound
	plu	1	Blended first sounds with added sound
	plai	1	Blended first sounds
	plait	0	Repeat word
trade	ch*	2	Articulation
	chai	1	Articulation
	chaid	0	Repeat word

*said by a student with a speech impairment who pronounces /th/ for /s/ and /w/ for /l/

Phoneme Segmentation Fluency Practice Scoring Sheet

Word	*Student Response*	*Score*	*Rule/Note*
bet	/b/.../e/.../t/	/b/ /e/ /t/ ____/ 3	
	/b/.../et/	/b/ /e/ /t/ ____/ 3	
	/be/.../t/	/b/ /e/ /t/ ____/ 3	
	/be/.../e/.../et/	/b/ /e/ /t/ ____/ 3	
	/b/... (3 seconds)	/b/ /e/ /t/ ____/ 3	
	/b/...bet	/b/ /e/ /t/ ____/ 3	
	bet	/b/ /e/ /t/ ____/ 3	
	/b/.../e/.../k/	/b/ /e/ /t/ ____/ 3	
	/b/.../e/.../s/.../t/	/b/ /e/ /t/ ____/ 3	
	/b/.../es/.../t/	/b/ /e/ /t/ ____/ 3	
slip	slip	/s/ /l/ /i/ /p/ ____/4	
	/sli/.../ip/	/s/ /l/ /i/ /p/ ____/4	
	/s/.../li/.../p/	/s/ /l/ /i/ /p/ ____/4	
	/sl/.../ip/	/s/ /l/ /i/ /p/ ____/4	
	/s/.../l/.../i/.../p/	/s/ /l/ /i/ /p/ ____/4	
	/s/...slip	/s/ /l/ /i/ /p/ ____/4	
	/s/.../l/...(3 seconds)	/s/ /l/ /i/ /p/ ____/4	
	/s/.../l/.../i/.../k/	/s/ /l/ /i/ /p/ ____/4	
	/s/.../l/.../i/.../p/.../s/	/s/ /l/ /i/ /p/ ____/4	
	/su/.../u/.../i/.../pu/	/s/ /l/ /i/ /p/ ____/4	
	/sk/.../i/.../p/	/s/ /l/ /i/ /p/ ____/4	
	/th/.../w/.../i/.../p/ *	/s/ /l/ /i/ /p/ ____/4	

*said by a student with a speech impairment who pronounces /th/ for /s/ and /w/ for /l/

Phoneme Segmentation Fluency Practice Scoring Sheet: Answer Key

Word	Student Response	Score	Rule/Note
bet	/b/.../e/.../t/	/b/ /e/ /t/ 3 / 3	Complete, correct segmentation
	/b/.../et/	/b/ /e/ /t/ 2 / 3	Partial segmentation
	/be/.../t/	/b/ /e/ /t/ 2 / 3	Partial segmentation
	/be/.../e/.../et/	/b/ /e/ /t/ 3 / 3	Overlapping segmentation
	/b/... (3 seconds)	/b/ /e/ /t/ 1 / 3	Partial segmentation
	/b/...bet	/b/ /e/ /t/ 1 / 3	Partial segmentation/repeat word
	bet	/b/ /e/ /t/ 0 / 3	Repeat word
	/b/.../e/.../k/	/b/ /e/ /t/ 2 / 3	Incorrect sound
	/b/.../e/.../s/.../t/	/b/ /e/ /t/ 3 / 3	Added sound
	/b/.../es/.../t/	/b/ /e/ /t/ 2 / 3	Incorrect sound
slip	slip	/s/ /l/ /i/ /p/ 0 /4	Repeat word
	/sli/.../ip/	/s/ /l/ /i/ /p/ 2 /4	Overlapping segmentation
	/s/.../li/.../p/	/s/ /l/ /i/ /p/ 3 /4	Partial segmentation
	/sl/.../ip/	/s/ /l/ /i/ /p/ 2 /4	Incomplete segmentation
	/s/.../l/.../i/.../p/	/s/ /l/ /i/ /p/ 4 /4	Complete, correct segmentation
	/s/...slip	/s/ /l/ /i/ /p/ 1 /4	Partial segmentation/repeat word
	/s/.../l/...(3 seconds)	/s/ /l/ /i/ /p/ 2 /4	Partial segmentation
	/s/.../l/.../i/.../k/	/s/ /l/ /i/ /p/ 3 /4	Incorrect sound
	/s/.../l/.../i/.../p/.../s/	/s/ /l/ /i/ /p/ 4 /4	Added sound
	/su/.../lu/.../i/.../pu/	/s/ /l/ /i/ /p/ 4 /4	Complete, correct segmentation with schwa sound
	/sk/.../i/.../p/	/s/ /l/ /i/ /p/ 2 /4	Incorrect sound
	/th/.../w/.../i/.../p/ *	/s/ /l/ /i/ /p/ 4 /4	Articulation

*said by a student with a speech impairment who pronounces /th/ for /s/ and /w/ for /l/

Nonsense Word Fluency Practice Scoring Sheet

Word	***Student Response***	***Score***	CLS	WWR	***Rule/Note***
dif	/d/.../i/.../f/	d i f	____/3	____	
	/du/.../i/.../fu/	d i f	____/3	____	
	/dif/	d i f	____/3	____	
	/d/.../i/.../f/.../dif/	d i f	____/3	____	
	/d/.../if/	d i f	____/3	____	
	/di/.../f/	d i f	____/3	____	
	/b/.../i/.../f/	d i f	____/3	____	
	/bif/	d i f	____/3	____	
	/di/.../f/.../dif/	d i f	____/3	____	
	/fid/	d i f	____/3	____	
	/fed/	d i f	____/3	____	
	/dief/	d i f	____/3	____	
	/d/.../f/	d i f	____/3	____	
	/d/.../d/.../d/.../i/.../f/	d i f	____/3	____	
	/d/.../i/.../f/.../t/	d i f	____/3	____	
	/dift/	d i f	____/3	____	
	/i/.../d/.../f/... (while correctly pointing to each letter)	d i f	____/3	____	
	/d/.../i/.../th/... (articulation error)	d i f	____/3	____	

Nonsense Word Fluency Practice Scoring Sheet: Answer Key

Word	Student Response	Score	CLS	WWR	Rule/Note
dif	/d/.../i/.../f/	d i f	3 /3	0	Correct letter sounds–sound by sound
	/du/.../i/.../fu/	d i f	3 /3	0	Students are not penalized for adding the schwa sound after consonants
	/dif/	d i f	3 /3	1	Correct letter sounds–recoded (read) as a word
	/d/.../i/.../f/.../dif/	d i f	3 /3	0	Correct sound by sound and then recoded
	/d/.../if/	d i f	3 /3	0	Correct letter sounds–onset-rime
	/di/.../f/	d i f	3 /3	0	Correct letter sounds
	/b/.../i/.../f/	d i f	2 /3	0	Incorrect letter sound–sound by sound
	/bif/	d i f	2 /3	0	Incorrect letter sound–recoded (read) as a word
	/di/.../f/.../dif/	d i f	3 /3	0	Correct letter sounds then recoded
	/fid/	d i f	1 /3	0	Correct letter sounds but read out of order
	/fed/	d i f	0 /3	0	Incorrect letter sounds
	/dief/	d i f	2 /3	0	Incorrect letter sound–all vowels should be read as short sound
	/d/.../f/	d i f	2 /3	0	Omitted sound
	/d/.../d/.../d/.../i/.../f/	d i f	3 /3	0	Repeating correct letter sound
	/d/.../i/.../f/.../t/	d i f	3 /3	0	Inserted sound–sound by sound
	/dift/	d i f	3 /3	0	Inserted sound–read as a word
	/i/.../d/.../f/... (while correctly pointing to each letter)	d i f	3 /3	0	Correct letter sound–read out of order, but credit can be given if the student points
	/d/.../i/.../th/... (articulation error)	d i f	3 /3	0	No penalty in scoring for articulation errors

DIBELS Oral Reading Fluency/Retell Practice Scoring Sheet

Passage

Four baskets were filled with fish. Now it was time to take them to the market. Ken helped his father load the baskets onto the family's boat. Ken's family lived on a large island off the coast of Africa. They used the boat to sail to market.

Student Response

Four buckets were fixed with big fish. Now it is time to take to the m…m…mar…(3 seconds, assessor says ***market***). Ken helped her father /l/ /oa/ /d/ the buckets the onto the f…f…fa…(3 seconds, assessor says ***family's***) boat. Ken's family lived on a large iceland off the (assessor says ***Stop***).

Score

Going to Market

0	Four baskets were filled with fish. Now it was time to take them to	14
14	the market. Ken helped his father load the baskets onto the family's boat.	27
27	Ken's family lived on a large island off the coast of Africa. They used the	42
42	boat to sail to market.	47

Total words: ________

Errors (include skipped words): – ________

Words correct: = ________

Retell: Student Response

They had a boat. And they went fishing.

Retell: Score

0 1 2 3 4 5 6 7 8 9	10	11	12	13	14	15	16	17	18	19	20	21	22	23	24	25
26	27	28	29	30	31	32	33	34	35	36	37	38	39	40	41	42 43 44 45 46 47 48

Retell Total: __________

DIBELS Oral Reading Fluency/Retell Practice Scoring Sheet: Answer Key

Passage

Four baskets were filled with fish. Now it was time to take them to the market. Ken helped his father load the baskets onto the family's boat. Ken's family lived on a large island off the coast of Africa. They used the boat to sail to market.

Student Response

Four buckets were fixed with big fish. Now it is time to take to the m…m…mar…(3 seconds, assessor says ***market***). Ken helped her father /l/ /oa/ /d/ the buckets the onto the f…f…fa…(3 seconds, assessor says ***family's***) boat. Ken's family lived on a large iceland off the (assessor says ***Stop***).

Score

Going to Market

0	Four ~~baskets~~ were ~~filled~~ with fish. Now it ~~was~~ time to take ~~them~~ to	14
14	the ~~market~~. Ken helped ~~his~~ father ~~load~~ the ~~baskets~~ onto the ~~family's~~ boat.	27
27	Ken's family lived on a large ~~island~~ off the] coast of Africa. They used the	42
42	boat to sail to market.	47

Total words: 36

Errors (include skipped words): – 10

Words correct: = 26

Retell: Student Response

They had a boat. And they went fishing.

Retell: Score

~~0~~	~~1~~	~~2~~	~~3~~	~~4~~	~~5~~	~~6~~	~~7~~	(8)	9	10	11	12	13	14	15	16	17	18	19	20	21	22	23	24	25
26	27	28	29	30	31	32	33	34	35	36	37	38	39	40	41	42	43	44	45	46	47	48			

Retell Total: 8

Appendix 3: Assessment Accuracy Checklists

These checklists are designed to be a tool for training and for conducting reliability checks on *DIBELS* assessors. They should be used to provide feedback to *DIBELS* assessors about their accuracy and consistency with standardized administration and scoring procedures. Additional information about conducting reliability checks can be found in *Chapter 4: Implementing* DIBELS Next *in Your School*. These Assessment Accuracy Checklists are discussed on pages 33 and 34.

FSF Assessment Accuracy Checklist

Consistently	Needs practice	Does the assessor:
☐	☐	1. Position materials so that student cannot see what is being recorded?
☐	☐	2. State standardized directions exactly as written? Practice item #1) ***Listen to me say this word, "man." The first sound that you hear in the word "man" is /mmm/. Listen. /mmm/. "Man." What is the first sound you hear in the word "man"?*** Correct: ***Good. /mmm/ is the first sound in "man."*** Incorrect: ***/mmm/ is the first sound you hear in the word "man." Listen. /mmm/. "Man." Say it with me. /mmm/. Let's try it again. What is the first sound you hear in the word "man"?*** Practice item #2) ***Listen to me say another word, "moon." What is the first sound you hear in the word "moon"?*** Correct: ***Good. /mmm/ is the first sound in "moon."*** Incorrect: ***/mmm/ is the first sound you hear in the word "moon." Listen. /mmm/. "moon." Say it with me. /mmm/. Let's try it again. What is the first sound you hear in the word "moon"?*** Practice item #3) ***Let's try another word, "sun."*** (Pause.) ***If the student does not respond, ask, What is the first sound you hear in the word "sun"?*** Correct: ***Good. /sss/ is the first sound in "sun."*** Incorrect: ***/sss/ is the first sound you hear in the word "sun." Listen. /sss/. "sun." Say it with me. /sss/. Let's try it again. What is the first sound you hear in the word "sun"?*** Begin testing. ***Now I am going to say more words. You tell me the first sound you hear in the word.*** (Say the first word from the list in the scoring booklet.)
☐	☐	3. Start the timer after saying the first word?
☐	☐	4. Use reminder procedures correctly and appropriately?
☐	☐	5. Say the next word immediately after the student responds?
☐	☐	6. Slash the zero if the student does not respond within 3 seconds on any word, and then read the next word?
☐	☐	7. Write "sc" above the slashed zero and circle any correct sounds if the student self-corrects within 3 seconds?
☐	☐	8. Score student responses correctly according to the scoring rules?
☐	☐	9. Discontinue if the student gets a score of zero on the first five words?
☐	☐	10. Stop at the end of 1 minute?
☐	☐	11. Correctly add the number of sounds in the 2-point and 1-point columns?
☐	☐	12. Record the total number of correctly produced first sounds in 1 minute?
☐	☐	13. Transfer the score correctly from the scoring page to the cover page of the scoring booklet?

LNF Assessment Accuracy Checklist

Consistently	Needs practice	Does the assessor:
☐	☐	1. Position materials so that student cannot see what is being recorded?
☐	☐	2. State standardized directions exactly as written? ***I am going to show you some letters. I want you to point to each letter and say its name.*** Begin testing. ***Start here*** (point to the first letter at the top of the page)***. Go this way*** (sweep your finger across the first two rows of letters) ***and say each letter name. Put your finger under the first letter*** (point)***. Ready, begin.***
☐	☐	3. Start the timer after saying ***Begin***?
☐	☐	4. Score student responses correctly according to the scoring rules?
☐	☐	5. Use reminder procedures correctly and appropriately?
☐	☐	6. Apply the 3-second wait rule (if the student does not name a letter after 3 seconds), slash the letter, provide the correct letter name, and point to the next letter if necessary?
☐	☐	7. Write "sc" above any letter that was previously slashed if the student self-corrects within 3 seconds?
☐	☐	8. Discontinue if the student gets a score of zero on the first row?
☐	☐	9. Place a bracket (]) at the 1-minute mark and say ***Stop***?
☐	☐	10. Correctly add the total number of correctly named letters?
☐	☐	11. Transfer the score correctly from the scoring page to the cover page of the scoring booklet?

PSF Assessment Accuracy Checklist

Consistently	Needs practice	Does the assessor:
☐	☐	1. Position materials so that student cannot see what is being recorded?
☐	☐	2. Read standardized directions exactly as written? ***We are going to say the sounds in words. Listen to me say all the sounds in the word "fan." /f/ /a/ /n/. Listen to another word,*** (pause) ***"jump." /j/ /u/ /m/ /p/. Your turn. Say all the sounds in "soap."*** Correct: ***Very good saying all the sounds in "soap."*** Incorrect: ***I said "soap" so you say /s/ /oa/ /p/. Your turn. Say all the sounds in "soap."*** Begin testing. ***I am going to say more words. I will say the word and you say all the sounds in the word.*** (Say the first word from the list in the scoring booklet.)
☐	☐	3. Start the timer after saying the first word?
☐	☐	4. Say the next word immediately after the student responds?
☐	☐	5. Say the next word if the student fails to say a sound within 3 seconds?
☐	☐	6. Discontinue if the student gets a score of zero on the first five words?
☐	☐	7. Use reminder procedures correctly and appropriately?
☐	☐	8. Write "sc" above any correct sound segments that were previously slashed if the student self-corrects within 3 seconds?
☐	☐	9. Score student responses correctly according to the scoring rules?
☐	☐	10. Place a bracket (]) at the 1-minute mark and tell the student to stop?
☐	☐	11. Correctly add the number of correct sound segments for each row?
☐	☐	12. Correctly add the total number of sound segments?
☐	☐	13. Transfer the score correctly from the scoring page to the front cover of the scoring booklet?

NWF Assessment Accuracy Checklist

Consistently	Needs practice	Does the assessor:
☐	☐	1. Position materials so that student cannot see what is being recorded?
☐	☐	2. State standardized directions exactly as written? ***We are going to read some make-believe words. Listen. This word is "sog."*** (Run your finger under the word as you say it.) ***The sounds are /s/ /o/ /g/*** (point to each letter)***. Your turn. Read this make-believe word*** (point to the word "mip")***. If you can't read the whole word, tell me any sounds you know.*** Correct ("mip"): ***Very good reading the word "mip."*** Correct (letter sounds): ***Very good. /m/ /i/ /p/*** (point to each letter) ***or "mip."*** Incorrect: ***Listen. /m/ /i/ /p/ or "mip."*** (Run your finger under the word as you say it.) ***Your turn. Read this make-believe word.*** (Point to the word "mip.") ***If you can't read the whole word, tell me any sounds you know.*** Begin testing. ***I would like you to read more make-believe words. Do your best reading. If you can't read the whole word, tell me any sounds you know.*** (Place the student copy in front of the student.) ***Put your finger under the first word. Ready, begin.***
☐	☐	3. Start the timer after saying ***Begin***?
☐	☐	4. Score student responses correctly according to the scoring rules?
☐	☐	5. Use reminder procedures correctly and appropriately?
☐	☐	6. Wait 3 seconds for the student to respond? If the student responds sound-by-sound, mixes sounds and words, or sounds out and recodes, allow 3 seconds, then provide the correct letter sound? If the student responds with whole words, allow 3 seconds, then provide the correct word?
☐	☐	7. Write "sc" above any previously slashed letter or word if the student self-corrects within 3 seconds?
☐	☐	8. Discontinue if the student gets a score of 0 for the first row?
☐	☐	9. Place a bracket (]) at the 1-minute mark and tell the student to stop?
☐	☐	10. Correctly add the correct letter sounds in each row?
☐	☐	11. Correctly add the total number of correct letter sounds and record it at the bottom of the scoring page?
☐	☐	12. Correctly add the correct whole words read in each row?
☐	☐	13. Correctly add the total number of whole words read and record it at the bottom of the scoring page?
☐	☐	14. Transfer both scores correctly from the scoring page to the front cover of the scoring booklet?

DORF Assessment Accuracy Checklist

Consistently	Needs practice	Does the assessor:
☐	☐	1. Position materials so that student cannot see what is being recorded?
☐	☐	2. State standardized directions exactly as written? ***I would like you to read a story to me. Please do your best reading. If you do not know a word, I will read the word for you. Keep reading until I say "stop." Be ready to tell me all about the story when you finish.*** (Place the passage in front of the student.) Begin testing. ***Put your finger under the first word*** (point to the first word of the passage)**.** ***Ready, begin.*** Begin testing (2nd and 3rd passages). ***Now read this story to me. Please do your best reading. Ready, begin.***
☐	☐	3. Start the timer when the student reads the first word of the passage?
☐	☐	4. Score student responses correctly according to the scoring rules?
☐	☐	5. Use reminder procedures correctly and appropriately?
☐	☐	6. Say the word and put a slash over it if the student fails to say it correctly within 3 seconds?
☐	☐	7. Write "sc" above a previously slashed word if the student self-corrects within 3 seconds?
☐	☐	8. Discontinue if the student does not read any words correctly in the first row of the passage?
☐	☐	9. Place a bracket (]) after the last word the student read before the minute ran out and tell the student to stop?
☐	☐	10. Correctly calculate the total number of words read (correct and errors) and record it on the scoring page?
☐	☐	11. Correctly add the number of errors and record it on the scoring page?
☐	☐	12. Correctly subtract the errors from the total words and record the words correct on the scoring page?
☐	☐	13. Record both scores on the front cover of the scoring booklet?

DORF Assessment Accuracy Checklist: Retell

Consistently	Needs practice	Does the assessor:
☐	☐	14. Administer Retell if the student read 40 or more words correct?
☐	☐	15. Remove the passage and then state the standardized Retell directions exactly as written? ***Now tell me as much as you can about the story you just read. Ready, begin.***
☐	☐	16. Start the stopwatch after saying ***Begin***?
☐	☐	17. Use reminder procedures correctly and appropriately?
☐	☐	18. Mark the number or words in the student's response and circle the total number of words?
☐	☐	19. Tell the student to stop if he/she is still retelling at the end of one minute?
☐	☐	20. Record the number of correct words at the bottom of the scoring booklet?
☐	☐	21. Record the score on the front cover of the scoring booklet?

Daze Assessment Accuracy Checklist

Consistently	Needs practice	Does the assessor:
☐	☐	1. Make sure each student has the appropriate worksheet?
☐	☐	2. State standardized directions exactly as written? ***I am going to give you a worksheet. When you get your worksheet, please write your name at the top and put your pencil down.*** ***You are going to read a story with some missing words. For each missing word there will be a box with three words. Circle the word that makes the most sense in the story. Look at Practice 1.*** ***Listen. After playing in the dirt, Sam went*** (pause) ***home, summer, was*** (pause) ***to wash her hands. You should circle the word "home" because "home" makes the most sense in the story. Listen. After playing in the dirt, Sam went <u>home</u> to wash her hands.*** ***Now it is your turn. Read Practice 2 <u>silently</u>. When you come to a box, read all the words in the box and circle the word that makes the most sense in the story. When you are done, put your pencil down.*** After 30 seconds: ***Listen. On her way home, she*** (pause) ***chair, sleep, saw*** (pause) ***an ice cream truck. You should have circled "saw" because "saw" makes the most sense in the story. Listen. On her way home, she <u>saw</u> an ice cream truck.*** ***When I say "begin," turn the page over and start reading the story silently. When you come to a box, read all the words in the box and circle the word that makes the most sense in the story. Ready? Begin.***
☐	☐	3. Start the timer after saying ***Begin***?
☐	☐	4. Use reminder procedures correctly and appropriately?
☐	☐	5. Say ***Stop, Put your pencils down*** at the end of 3 minutes?
☐	☐	6. Use the scoring key correctly?
☐	☐	7. Add the number of correct and incorrect responses accurately?
☐	☐	8. Write the total number of correct responses on the "C" line of the worksheet cover page?
☐	☐	9. Write the total number of incorrect responses on the "I" line of the worksheet cover page?

Appendix 4: Sample Statement and Letters

The sample statement and letters in this appendix are discussed in *Chapter 4: Implementing* DIBELS Next *in Your School*, on page 40.

Sample Student Statement

The following is a sample statement that can be used to introduce students to *DIBELS* testing. The wording of this sample is meant to be used on the day the students will be tested. The statement can be modified to fit other situations.

This is only an example, and each school is encouraged to introduce *DIBELS* testing to students in a manner appropriate to the school community.

> Today we are going to do some activities that will help me know how to teach you better.
>
> I will be working with some of you, and some of you will go with *Mr. Jones, Ms. Smith, or Mrs. Thomas (replace with names of assessment team members).*
>
> We will go to quiet places such as the *cafeteria, the library, the nurse's office, or the gym (replace with correct locations).*
>
> We will ask you to
>
> Kindergarten: "Tell us letters and the sounds in words."
> First grade *(beginning of year)*: "Tell us letters and the sounds in words."
> First grade *(middle and end of year)*: "Tell us the sounds in words and read short stories."
> Second to sixth grade: "Read short stories and tell about them."
>
> Some of the activities may be easy, and some may be hard. I want you to concentrate and do your best. You will not get a grade on these activities, but you should do your best so I can know what I need to teach you next.

Sample Parent Announcement Letter

The following is a sample letter that can be used to introduce parents and guardians to *DIBELS* testing. Each school is encouraged to provide accurate and understandable information to parents and guardians in a manner appropriate to its school community.

Dear Parents and Guardians,

The teachers and administrators at our school are committed to helping your child become a successful reader. As part of this commitment, our school has chosen to use a test called *DIBELS* to help us examine how your child is doing in learning important reading skills.

DIBELS stands for *Dynamic Indicators of Basic Early Literacy Skills*. *DIBELS* tests four skills that are necessary for learning to read. Children who learn these skills become good readers. The skills are:

- **Phonemic Awareness:** Hearing and using sounds in spoken words
- **Phonics:** Knowing the sounds of the letters and sounding out written words
- **Accurate and Fluent Reading:** Reading stories and other materials easily and quickly with few mistakes
- **Reading Comprehension:** Understanding what is read

DIBELS is made up of six short individual tests. Because each test focuses on a different reading skill, your child may be given two to four *DIBELS* tests depending on his or her grade level.

Each test takes approximately 1 minute because the tests are used only as *indicators*. Much like using a thermometer to take a child's temperature is an indicator of overall health, each test is an indicator of how well a child is doing in learning a particular early reading skill. *DIBELS* is used to determine the reading skills of millions of children throughout the United States. The scores tell us whether a child is likely to be "on track" for learning to read or whether a child may need some help in learning important reading skills. Your child's teacher will use the information to better help your child. For example, a *DIBELS* test may tell us that we need to spend more time teaching your child how to "sound out" unknown words.

DIBELS is used to identify children who may need extra help to become good readers and check up on those children while they receive the extra help to make sure they are making progress. *DIBELS* also may be used to make decisions about how well our school's overall reading program is working for all children. *DIBELS* will not be used to grade your child.

We are working hard at school to make sure that every child is on target for success, and we thank you for your efforts at home. Together, we will help your child become a successful reader.

Sincerely,

(principal's name)

Sample Results Letter

The following is a sample letter that can be used to discuss *DIBELS* results with parents and guardians. Each school is encouraged to provide accurate and understandable information to parents and guardians in a manner appropriate to the school community.

Dear Parents of *(insert student name)*:

All students in our school are tested three times during the school year using the *Dynamic Indicators of Basic Early Literacy Skills* (*DIBELS*). The purpose of this assessment is to monitor your child's development in reading, to identify students needing additional help, and to guide the teacher's classroom instruction.

The *DIBELS* measures given in first grade are described below:

***DIBELS* Measure**	**Skill Area**	**Types of Activities**
Phoneme Segmentation Fluency	Phonemic Awareness	Saying individual sounds in words
Nonsense Word Fluency	Basic Phonics	Letter-sound correspondence and blending letter sounds into words
DIBELS Oral Reading Fluency	Accurate and Fluent Reading and Reading Comprehension	Accurately reading a passage of text and retelling what was read

In the last several weeks, we have tested all students to check their reading progress. Teachers will use this information, along with classroom information, to determine any areas in which students need more instruction.

Your child's results are provided on the next page.

The *DIBELS* Composite Score is a combination of multiple *DIBELS* scores and provides the best overall estimate of a student's reading proficiency. The scores used to calculate the composite vary by grade and time of year, so composite scores should be compared to the goal only at that time of the school year, and not to composite scores at other times of the year.

Please note that the goal number listed next to your child's score indicates the minimum target for students at the beginning, middle, and end of the school year.

Scores at or above the goal indicate that the student is on track for meeting future reading outcomes with the instruction that is currently being provided. Scores below the goal indicate that the student is currently not on track to meet future reading outcomes and may need additional reading support to catch up.

Students who score at or above the Composite Score goal may still need additional instruction in one or more skill areas, as indicated by a score below the goal on one of the *DIBELS* measures (Phoneme Segmentation Fluency, Nonsense Word Fluency, or *DIBELS* Oral Reading Fluency).

Sample Results Letter, continued

DIBELS Tests for First Grade	Fall Goal	Fall Score	Winter Goal	Winter Score	Spring Goal	Spring Score
DIBELS Composite Score	113		130		155	
Phoneme Segmentation Fluency	40		*not given*		*not given*	
Nonsense Word Fluency — CLS	27		43		58	
Nonsense Word Fluency — WWR	1		8		13	
DIBELS Oral Reading Fluency — Words Correct	*not given*		23		47	
DIBELS Oral Reading Fluency — Accuracy			78%		90%	
DIBELS Oral Reading Fluency — Retell			n/a		15	

Scores for your child indicate the following:

_________ Your child will receive the regular classroom reading instruction.

_________ Your child will receive additional instruction within the classroom on the following skills:

____

_________ Your child will be recommended for additional reading instruction outside the classroom on the following skills:

____

If you have any questions concerning your child's *DIBELS* information, please contact me or your child's teacher.

Sincerely,

(principal's name)

Appendix 5: Benchmark Goals and Cut Points for Risk

Benchmark Goals

DIBELS benchmark goals are empirically derived, criterion-referenced target scores that represent adequate reading progress. A benchmark goal indicates a level of skill at which the student is likely to achieve the next *DIBELS* benchmark goal or reading outcome. Benchmark goals for *DIBELS* are based on research that examines the predictive validity of a score on a measure at a particular point in time, compared to later *DIBELS* measures and external outcome assessments. If a student achieves a benchmark goal, then the odds are in favor of that student achieving later reading outcomes if he/she receives research-based instruction from a core classroom curriculum.

Benchmark Goal Research

The *DIBELS Next* benchmark goals, cut points for risk, and Composite Score were developed based upon data collected in a study conducted during the 2009–2010 school year. The goals represent a series of conditional probabilities of meeting later important reading outcomes. The external criterion was the Group Reading and Diagnostic Evaluation (GRADE; Williams, 2001). The 40th percentile on the GRADE assessment was used as an indicator that the student was making adequate progress in acquisition of important early reading and/or reading skills. Data for the study were collected in 13 elementary and middle schools in five states. Data collection included administering the *DIBELS Next* measures to participating students in grades K–6 in addition to the GRADE. Participants in the study were 3,816 students across grades K–6 from general education classrooms who were receiving English language reading instruction, including students with disabilities and students who were English language learners, provided they had the response capabilities to participate. The study included both students who were struggling in reading and those who were typically achieving. A subset of the total sample participated in the GRADE assessment (n = 1306 across grades K–6). Additional information about the study will be included in the *DIBELS Next Technical Manual*, which will be available in January, 2011.

Cut Points for Risk

The *cut points for risk* indicate a level of skill below which the student is unlikely to achieve subsequent reading goals without receiving additional, targeted instructional support. Students with scores below the cut point for risk are identified as likely to need intensive support. Intensive support refers to interventions that incorporate something more or something different from the core curriculum or supplemental support. Intensive support might entail:

- delivering instruction in a smaller group;
- providing more instructional time or more practice;
- presenting smaller skill steps in the instructional hierarchy;
- providing more explicit modeling and instruction; and/or
- providing greater scaffolding and practice.

Because students needing intensive support are likely to have individual and sometimes unique needs, we recommend that their progress be monitored frequently and their intervention modified dynamically to ensure adequate progress.

Between a benchmark goal and a cut point for risk is a range of scores that makes the student's future performance harder to predict. To ensure that the greatest number of students achieve later reading success, it is best for students with scores in this range to receive carefully targeted additional support in the skill areas where they are having difficulty, to be monitored regularly to ensure that they are making adequate progress, and to receive increased or modified support if necessary to achieve subsequent reading goals. This type of instructional support is referred to as strategic support.

Table A5.1 provides the target or design odds of achieving later reading outcomes and labels for likely need for support for each of the score levels. Benchmark goals and cut points for risk are provided for the *DIBELS* Composite Score as well as for individual *DIBELS* measures.

Table A5.1 Odds of Achieving Subsequent Early Literacy Goals, *DIBELS Next* Benchmark Goal Levels, and Likely Need for Support

Odds of achieving subsequent early literacy goals	Visual Representation	Score Level	Likely need for support to achieve subsequent early literacy goals
80% to 90%	■	At or Above Benchmark *scores at or above the benchmark goal*	Likely to Need Core Support
40% to 60%	◩	Below Benchmark *scores below the benchmark goal and at or above the cut point for risk*	Likely to Need Strategic Support
10% to 20%	□	Well Below Benchmark *scores below the cut point for risk*	Likely to Need Intensive Support

On the next page is an overview chart of the *DIBELS* benchmark goals and cut points for risk. Following the chart are grade-specific (K–6) lists of score ranges for each *DIBELS* measure.

DIBELS® Next: Summary of Benchmark Goals and Cut Points for Risk

Measure	Kindergarten			First Grade			Second Grade			Third Grade			Fourth Grade			Fifth Grade			Sixth Grade		
	Beg	Mid	End	Beg	Mid	End	Beg	Mid	End	Beg	Mid	End	Beg	Mid	End	Beg	Mid	End	Beg	Mid	End
DIBELS Composite Score	**26** / 13	**122** / 85	**119** / 89	**113** / 97	**130** / 100	**155** / 111	**141** / 109	**190** / 145	**238** / 180	**220** / 180	**285** / 235	**330** / 280	**290** / 245	**330** / 290	**391** / 330	**357** / 258	**372** / 310	**415** / 340	**344** / 280	**358** / 285	**380** / 324
First Sound Fluency (FSF)	**10** / 5	**30** / 20																			
Letter Naming Fluency (LNF)	No benchmark set for LNF																				
Phoneme Segmentation Fluency (PSF)		**20** / 10	**40** / 25	**40** / 25																	
Nonsense Word Fluency (NWF) Correct Letter Sounds		**17** / 8	**28** / 15	**27** / 18	**43** / 33	**58** / 47	**54** / 35														
NWF Whole Words Read				**1** / 0	**8** / 3	**13** / 6	**13** / 6														
DIBELS Oral Reading Fluency (DORF) Words Correct					**23** / 16	**47** / 32	**52** / 37	**72** / 55	**87** / 65	**70** / 55	**86** / 68	**100** / 80	**90** / 70	**103** / 79	**115** / 95	**111** / 96	**120** / 101	**130** / 105	**107** / 90	**109** / 92	**120** / 95
DORF Accuracy					**78%** / 68%	**90%** / 82%	**90%** / 81%	**96%** / 91%	**97%** / 93%	**95%** / 89%	**96%** / 92%	**97%** / 94%	**96%** / 93%	**97%** / 94%	**98%** / 95%	**98%** / 95%	**98%** / 96%	**99%** / 97%	**97%** / 94%	**97%** / 94%	**98%** / 96%
DORF Retell						**15** / 0	**16** / 8	**21** / 13	**27** / 18	**20** / 10	**26** / 18	**30** / 20	**27** / 14	**30** / 20	**33** / 24	**33** / 22	**36** / 25	**36** / 25	**27** / 16	**29** / 18	**32** / 24
DORF Retell Quality of Response								**2** / 1	**2** / 1	**2** / 1	**2** / 1	**3** / 2	**2** / 1	**2** / 1	**3** / 2	**2** / 1	**3** / 2	**3** / 2	**2** / 1	**2** / 1	**3** / 2
Daze										**8** / 5	**11** / 7	**19** / 14	**15** / 10	**17** / 12	**24** / 20	**18** / 12	**20** / 13	**24** / 18	**18** / 14	**19** / 14	**21** / 15

DIBELS Composite Score: A combination of multiple *DIBELS* scores, which provides the best overall estimate of the student's reading proficiency. For information on how to calculate the composite score, see the *DIBELS Next Benchmark Goals and Composite Score* document available from http://dibels.org/.

BENCHMARK GOAL (bold number at top of each box): Students scoring at or above the benchmark goal have the odds in their favor (approximately 80%–90%) of achieving later importing reading outcomes. These scores are identified as "At or Above Benchmark" and the students are likely to need *Core Support*.

CUT POINT FOR RISK (smaller number in each box): Students scoring below the cut point for risk are unlikely (approximately 10%–20%) to achieve subsequent goals without receiving additional, targeted instructional support. These scores are identified as "Well Below Benchmark" and the students are likely to need *Intensive Support*.

Scores below the benchmark goal and at or above the cut point for risk are identified as "Below Benchmark." In this range, a student's future performance is harder to predict, and these students are likely to need *Strategic Support*.

This page is adapted from a chart developed by Cache County School District.

Kindergarten Benchmark Goals and Cut Points for Risk

Measure	Score Level	Likely Need for Support	Beginning of Year	Middle of Year	End of Year
DIBELS Composite Score	At or Above Benchmark	Likely to Need Core Support	26 +	122 +	119 +
	Below Benchmark	Likely to Need Strategic Support	13 – 25	85 – 121	89 – 118
	Well Below Benchmark	Likely to Need Intensive Support	0 – 12	0 – 84	0 – 88
FSF	At or Above Benchmark	Likely to Need Core Support	10 +	30 +	
	Below Benchmark	Likely to Need Strategic Support	5 – 9	20 – 29	
	Well Below Benchmark	Likely to Need Intensive Support	0 – 4	0 – 19	
PSF	At or Above Benchmark	Likely to Need Core Support		20 +	40 +
	Below Benchmark	Likely to Need Strategic Support		10 – 19	25 – 39
	Well Below Benchmark	Likely to Need Intensive Support		0 – 9	0 – 24
NWF-CLS	At or Above Benchmark	Likely to Need Core Support		17 +	28 +
	Below Benchmark	Likely to Need Strategic Support		8 – 16	15 – 27
	Well Below Benchmark	Likely to Need Intensive Support		0 – 7	0 – 14

The benchmark goal is the number provided in the “At or Above Benchmark” row. The cut point for risk is the first number provided in the “Below Benchmark” row.

First Grade Benchmark Goals and Cut Points for Risk

Measure	Score Level	Likely Need for Support	Beginning of Year	Middle of Year	End of Year
DIBELS Composite Score	At or Above Benchmark	Likely to Need Core Support	113 +	130 +	155 +
	Below Benchmark	Likely to Need Strategic Support	97 – 112	100 – 129	111 – 154
	Well Below Benchmark	Likely to Need Intensive Support	0 – 96	0 – 99	0 – 110
PSF	At or Above Benchmark	Likely to Need Core Support	40 +		
	Below Benchmark	Likely to Need Strategic Support	25 – 39		
	Well Below Benchmark	Likely to Need Intensive Support	0 – 24		
NWF-CLS	At or Above Benchmark	Likely to Need Core Support	27 +	43 +	58 +
	Below Benchmark	Likely to Need Strategic Support	18 – 26	33 – 42	47 – 57
	Well Below Benchmark	Likely to Need Intensive Support	0 – 17	0 – 32	0 – 46
NWF-WWR	At or Above Benchmark	Likely to Need Core Support	1 +	8 +	13 +
	Below Benchmark	Likely to Need Strategic Support	0	3 – 7	6 – 12
	Well Below Benchmark	Likely to Need Intensive Support		0 – 2	0 – 5
DORF Words Correct	At or Above Benchmark	Likely to Need Core Support		23 +	47 +
	Below Benchmark	Likely to Need Strategic Support		16 – 22	32 – 46
	Well Below Benchmark	Likely to Need Intensive Support		0 – 15	0 – 31
DORF Accuracy	At or Above Benchmark	Likely to Need Core Support		78% +	90% +
	Below Benchmark	Likely to Need Strategic Support		68% – 77%	82% – 89%
	Well Below Benchmark	Likely to Need Intensive Support		0% – 67%	0% – 81%
Retell	At or Above Benchmark	Likely to Need Core Support			15 +
	Below Benchmark	Likely to Need Strategic Support			0 – 14
	Well Below Benchmark	Likely to Need Intensive Support			

The benchmark goal is the number provided in the “At or Above Benchmark” row. The cut point for risk is the first number provided in the “Below Benchmark” row.

Second Grade Benchmark Goals and Cut Points for Risk

Measure	Score Level	Likely Need for Support	Beginning of Year	Middle of Year	End of Year
DIBELS Composite Score	At or Above Benchmark	Likely to Need Core Support	141 +	190 +	238 +
	Below Benchmark	Likely to Need Strategic Support	109 – 140	145 – 189	180 – 237
	Well Below Benchmark	Likely to Need Intensive Support	0 – 108	0 – 144	0 – 179
NWF-CLS	At or Above Benchmark	Likely to Need Core Support	54 +		
	Below Benchmark	Likely to Need Strategic Support	35 – 53		
	Well Below Benchmark	Likely to Need Intensive Support	0 – 34		
NWF-WWR	At or Above Benchmark	Likely to Need Core Support	13 +		
	Below Benchmark	Likely to Need Strategic Support	6 – 12		
	Well Below Benchmark	Likely to Need Intensive Support	0 – 5		
DORF Words Correct	At or Above Benchmark	Likely to Need Core Support	52 +	72 +	87 +
	Below Benchmark	Likely to Need Strategic Support	37 – 51	55 – 71	65 – 86
	Well Below Benchmark	Likely to Need Intensive Support	0 – 36	0 – 54	0 – 64
DORF Accuracy	At or Above Benchmark	Likely to Need Core Support	90% +	96% +	97% +
	Below Benchmark	Likely to Need Strategic Support	81% – 89%	91% – 95%	93% – 96%
	Well Below Benchmark	Likely to Need Intensive Support	0% – 80%	0% – 90%	0% – 92%
Retell	At or Above Benchmark	Likely to Need Core Support	16 +	21 +	27 +
	Below Benchmark	Likely to Need Strategic Support	8 – 15	13 – 20	18 – 26
	Well Below Benchmark	Likely to Need Intensive Support	0 – 7	0 – 12	0 – 17
Retell Quality of Response	At or Above Benchmark	Likely to Need Core Support		2 +	2 +
	Below Benchmark	Likely to Need Strategic Support		1	1
	Well Below Benchmark	Likely to Need Intensive Support			

The benchmark goal is the number provided in the “At or Above Benchmark” row. The cut point for risk is the first number provided in the “Below Benchmark” row.

Third Grade Benchmark Goals and Cut Points for Risk

Measure	Score Level	Likely Need for Support	Beginning of Year	Middle of Year	End of Year
DIBELS Composite Score	At or Above Benchmark	Likely to Need Core Support	220 +	285 +	330 +
	Below Benchmark	Likely to Need Strategic Support	180 – 219	235 – 284	280 – 329
	Well Below Benchmark	Likely to Need Intensive Support	0 – 179	0 – 234	0 – 279
DORF Words Correct	At or Above Benchmark	Likely to Need Core Support	70 +	86 +	100 +
	Below Benchmark	Likely to Need Strategic Support	55 – 69	68 – 85	80 – 99
	Well Below Benchmark	Likely to Need Intensive Support	0 – 54	0 – 67	0 – 79
DORF Accuracy	At or Above Benchmark	Likely to Need Core Support	95% +	96% +	97% +
	Below Benchmark	Likely to Need Strategic Support	89% – 94%	92% – 95%	94% – 96%
	Well Below Benchmark	Likely to Need Intensive Support	0% – 88%	0% – 91%	0% – 93%
Retell	At or Above Benchmark	Likely to Need Core Support	20 +	26 +	30 +
	Below Benchmark	Likely to Need Strategic Support	10 – 19	18 – 25	20 – 29
	Well Below Benchmark	Likely to Need Intensive Support	0 – 9	0 – 17	0 – 19
Retell Quality of Response	At or Above Benchmark	Likely to Need Core Support	2 +	2 +	3 +
	Below Benchmark	Likely to Need Strategic Support	1	1	2
	Well Below Benchmark	Likely to Need Intensive Support			1
Daze Adjusted Score	At or Above Benchmark	Likely to Need Core Support	8 +	11 +	19 +
	Below Benchmark	Likely to Need Strategic Support	5 – 7	7 – 10	14 – 18
	Well Below Benchmark	Likely to Need Intensive Support	0 – 4	0 – 6	0 – 13

The benchmark goal is the number provided in the “At or Above Benchmark” row. The cut point for risk is the first number provided in the “Below Benchmark” row.

Fourth Grade Benchmark Goals and Cut Points for Risk

Measure	Score Level	Likely Need for Support	Beginning of Year	Middle of Year	End of Year
DIBELS Composite Score	At or Above Benchmark	Likely to Need Core Support	290 +	330 +	391 +
	Below Benchmark	Likely to Need Strategic Support	245 – 289	290 – 329	330 – 390
	Well Below Benchmark	Likely to Need Intensive Support	0 – 244	0 – 289	0 – 329
DORF Words Correct	At or Above Benchmark	Likely to Need Core Support	90 +	103 +	115 +
	Below Benchmark	Likely to Need Strategic Support	70 – 89	79 – 102	95 – 114
	Well Below Benchmark	Likely to Need Intensive Support	0 – 69	0 – 78	0 – 94
DORF Accuracy	At or Above Benchmark	Likely to Need Core Support	96% +	97% +	98% +
	Below Benchmark	Likely to Need Strategic Support	93% – 95%	94% – 96%	95% – 97%
	Well Below Benchmark	Likely to Need Intensive Support	0% – 92%	0% – 93%	0% – 94%
Retell	At or Above Benchmark	Likely to Need Core Support	27 +	30 +	33 +
	Below Benchmark	Likely to Need Strategic Support	14 – 26	20 – 29	24 – 32
	Well Below Benchmark	Likely to Need Intensive Support	0 – 13	0 – 19	0 – 23
Retell Quality of Response	At or Above Benchmark	Likely to Need Core Support	2 +	2 +	3 +
	Below Benchmark	Likely to Need Strategic Support	1	1	2
	Well Below Benchmark	Likely to Need Intensive Support			1
Daze Adjusted Score	At or Above Benchmark	Likely to Need Core Support	15 +	17 +	24 +
	Below Benchmark	Likely to Need Strategic Support	10 – 14	12 – 16	20 – 23
	Well Below Benchmark	Likely to Need Intensive Support	0 – 9	0 – 11	0 – 19

The benchmark goal is the number provided in the “At or Above Benchmark” row. The cut point for risk is the first number provided in the “Below Benchmark” row.

Fifth Grade Benchmark Goals and Cut Points for Risk

Measure	Score Level	Likely Need for Support	Beginning of Year	Middle of Year	End of Year
DIBELS Composite Score	At or Above Benchmark	Likely to Need Core Support	357 +	372 +	415 +
	Below Benchmark	Likely to Need Strategic Support	258 – 356	310 – 371	340 – 414
	Well Below Benchmark	Likely to Need Intensive Support	0 – 257	0 – 309	0 – 339
DORF Words Correct	At or Above Benchmark	Likely to Need Core Support	111 +	120 +	130 +
	Below Benchmark	Likely to Need Strategic Support	96 – 110	101 – 119	105 – 129
	Well Below Benchmark	Likely to Need Intensive Support	0 – 95	0 – 100	0 – 104
DORF Accuracy	At or Above Benchmark	Likely to Need Core Support	98% +	98% +	99% +
	Below Benchmark	Likely to Need Strategic Support	95% – 97%	96% – 97%	97% – 98%
	Well Below Benchmark	Likely to Need Intensive Support	0% – 94%	0% – 95%	0% – 96%
Retell	At or Above Benchmark	Likely to Need Core Support	33 +	36 +	36 +
	Below Benchmark	Likely to Need Strategic Support	22 – 32	25 – 35	25 – 35
	Well Below Benchmark	Likely to Need Intensive Support	0 – 21	0 – 24	0 – 24
Retell Quality of Response	At or Above Benchmark	Likely to Need Core Support	2 +	3 +	3 +
	Below Benchmark	Likely to Need Strategic Support	1	2	2
	Well Below Benchmark	Likely to Need Intensive Support		1	1
Daze Adjusted Score	At or Above Benchmark	Likely to Need Core Support	18 +	20 +	24 +
	Below Benchmark	Likely to Need Strategic Support	12 – 17	13 – 19	18 – 23
	Well Below Benchmark	Likely to Need Intensive Support	0 – 11	0 – 12	0 – 17

The benchmark goal is the number provided in the "At or Above Benchmark" row. The cut point for risk is the first number provided in the "Below Benchmark" row.

Sixth Grade Benchmark Goals and Cut Points for Risk

Measure	Score Level	Likely Need for Support	Beginning of Year	Middle of Year	End of Year
DIBELS Composite Score	At or Above Benchmark	Likely to Need Core Support	344 +	358 +	380 +
	Below Benchmark	Likely to Need Strategic Support	280 – 343	285 – 357	324 – 379
	Well Below Benchmark	Likely to Need Intensive Support	0 – 279	0 – 284	0 – 323
DORF Words Correct	At or Above Benchmark	Likely to Need Core Support	107 +	109 +	120 +
	Below Benchmark	Likely to Need Strategic Support	90 – 106	92 – 108	95 – 119
	Well Below Benchmark	Likely to Need Intensive Support	0 – 89	0 – 91	0 – 94
DORF Accuracy	At or Above Benchmark	Likely to Need Core Support	97% +	97% +	98% +
	Below Benchmark	Likely to Need Strategic Support	94% – 96%	94% – 96%	96% – 97%
	Well Below Benchmark	Likely to Need Intensive Support	0% – 93%	0% – 93%	0% – 95%
Retell	At or Above Benchmark	Likely to Need Core Support	27 +	29 +	32 +
	Below Benchmark	Likely to Need Strategic Support	16 – 26	18 – 28	24 – 31
	Well Below Benchmark	Likely to Need Intensive Support	0 – 15	0 – 17	0 – 23
Retell Quality of Response	At or Above Benchmark	Likely to Need Core Support	2 +	2 +	3 +
	Below Benchmark	Likely to Need Strategic Support	1	1	2
	Well Below Benchmark	Likely to Need Intensive Support			1
Daze Adjusted Score	At or Above Benchmark	Likely to Need Core Support	18 +	19 +	21 +
	Below Benchmark	Likely to Need Strategic Support	14 – 17	14 – 18	15 – 20
	Well Below Benchmark	Likely to Need Intensive Support	0 – 13	0 – 13	0 – 14

The benchmark goal is the number provided in the "At or Above Benchmark" row. The cut point for risk is the first number provided in the "Below Benchmark" row.

Appendix 6: *DIBELS* Composite Score

The *DIBELS* Composite Score is a combination of multiple *DIBELS* scores and provides the best overall estimate of the student's early literacy skills and/or reading proficiency. Most data-management services will calculate the *DIBELS* Composite Score for you. To calculate the *DIBELS* Composite Score yourself, see the *DIBELS Next* Composite Score Worksheets on the following pages. In *DIBELS 6th Edition*, the Instructional Recommendations provided the best overall estimate of a student's early literacy skills and/or reading proficiency. The *DIBELS Next* Composite Score and the benchmark goals and cut points for risk based on the composite score replace the Instructional Recommendations on *DIBELS 6th Edition*.

Benchmark goals and cut points for risk for the *DIBELS* Composite Score are based on the same logic and procedures as the individual *DIBELS* measures; however, since the DIBELS Composite Score provides the best overall estimate of a student's skills, the *DIBELS* Composite Score should generally be interpreted first. If a student is at or above the benchmark goal on the *DIBELS* Composite Score, the odds are in the student's favor of reaching later important reading outcomes. Some students who score at or above the *DIBELS* Composite Score benchmark goal may still need additional support in one of the basic early literacy skills, as indicated by a below benchmark score on an individual *DIBELS Next* measure (FSF, PSF, NWF, DORF, or Daze), especially for students whose composite score is close to the benchmark goal.

Because the scores used to calculate the *DIBELS* Composite Score vary by grade and time of school year, it is important to note that the composite score generally cannot be used to directly measure growth over time or to compare results across grades or times of year. However, because the logic and procedures used to establish benchmark goals are consistent across grades and times of the school year, the percent of students at or above benchmark can be compared, even though the mean scores are not comparable.

K Kindergarten DIBELS® Next Composite Score Worksheet

The *DIBELS* Composite Score is used to interpret student results for *DIBELS Next*. Most data-management services will calculate the composite score for you. If you do not use a data-management service or if your data-management service does not calculate it, you can use this worksheet to calculate the composite score.

Name: ______________________ **Class:** ______________________

Beginning of Year Benchmark

FSF Score = ______________ [1]

LNF Score = ______________ [2]

DIBELS Composite Score (add values 1–2) = ______

Do not calculate the composite score if any of the values are missing.

Middle of Year Benchmark

FSF Score = ______________ [1]

LNF Score = ______________ [2]

PSF Score = ______________ [3]

NWF CLS Score = ______________ [4]

DIBELS Composite Score (add values 1–4) = ______

Do not calculate the composite score if any of the values are missing.

End of Year Benchmark

LNF Score = ______________ [1]

PSF Score = ______________ [2]

NWF CLS Score = ______________ [3]

DIBELS Composite Score (add values 1–3) = ______

Do not calculate the composite score if any of the values are missing.

1 First Grade DIBELS® Next Composite Score Worksheet

© Dynamic Measurement Group, Inc. / August 31, 2010

The *DIBELS* Composite Score is used to interpret student results for *DIBELS Next*. Most data-management services will calculate the composite score for you. If you do not use a data-management service or if your data-management service does not calculate it, you can use this worksheet to calculate the composite score.

Name: ______________________ **Class:** ______________________

Beginning of Year Benchmark

LNF Score = ______________ [1]

PSF Score = ______________ [2]

NWF CLS Score = ______________ [3]

DIBELS Composite Score (add values 1–3) = [ ]

Do not calculate the composite score if any of the values are missing.

Middle of Year Benchmark

NWF CLS Score = ______________ [1]

NWF WWR Score = ______________ [2]

DORF Words Correct = ______________ [3]

DORF Accuracy Percent: ________ %

100 x (Words Correct / Words Correct + Errors)

Accuracy Value from Table = ______________ [4]

DIBELS Composite Score (add values 1–4) = [ ]

Do not calculate the composite score if any of the values are missing.

Middle of Year	
DORF Accuracy Percent	Accuracy Value
0% – 49%	0
50% – 52%	2
53% – 55%	8
56% – 58%	14
59% – 61%	20
62% – 64%	26
65% – 67%	32
68% – 70%	38
71% – 73%	44
74% – 76%	50
77% – 79%	56
80% – 82%	62
83% – 85%	68
86% – 88%	74
89% – 91%	80
92% – 94%	86
95% – 97%	92
98% – 100%	98

End of Year Benchmark

NWF WWR Score ________ **x 2** = ______________ [1]

DORF Words Correct = ______________ [2]

DORF Accuracy Percent: ________ %

100 x (Words Correct / Words Correct + Errors)

Accuracy Value from Table = ______________ [3]

DIBELS Composite Score (add values 1–3) = [ ]

Do not calculate the composite score if any of the values are missing.

End of Year	
DORF Accuracy Percent	Accuracy Value
0% – 64%	0
65% – 66%	3
67% – 68%	9
69% – 70%	15
71% – 72%	21
73% – 74%	27
75% – 76%	33
77% – 78%	39
79% – 80%	45
81% – 82%	51
83% – 84%	57
85% – 86%	63
87% – 88%	69
89% – 90%	75
91% – 92%	81
93% – 94%	87
95% – 96%	93
97% – 98%	99
99% – 100%	105

2 Second Grade DIBELS® Next Composite Score Worksheet

© Dynamic Measurement Group, Inc. / August 31, 2010

The *DIBELS* Composite Score is used to interpret student results for *DIBELS Next*. Most data-management services will calculate the composite score for you. If you do not use a data-management service or if your data-management service does not calculate it, you can use this worksheet to calculate the composite score.

Name: ______________________ **Class:** ______________________

Beginning of Year	
DORF Accuracy Percent	Accuracy Value
0% – 64%	0
65% – 66%	3
67% – 68%	9
69% – 70%	15
71% – 72%	21
73% – 74%	27
75% – 76%	33
77% – 78%	39
79% – 80%	45
81% – 82%	51
83% – 84%	57
85% – 86%	63
87% – 88%	69
89% – 90%	75
91% – 92%	81
93% – 94%	87
95% – 96%	93
97% – 98%	99
99% – 100%	105

Middle and End of Year	
DORF Accuracy Percent	Accuracy Value
0% – 85%	0
86%	8
87%	16
88%	24
89%	32
90%	40
91%	48
92%	56
93%	64
94%	72
95%	80
96%	88
97%	96
98%	104
99%	112
100%	120

Beginning of Year Benchmark

NWF WWR Score __________ **x 2** = ____________________ [1]

DORF Words Correct = ____________________ [2]

DORF Accuracy Percent: ________ %

100 x (Words Correct / Words Correct + Errors)

Accuracy Value from Table = ____________________ [3]

DIBELS Composite Score (add values 1–3) = [ ]

Do not calculate the composite score if any of the values are missing.

Middle of Year Benchmark

DORF Words Correct = ____________________ [1]

Retell Score __________ **x 2** = ____________________ [2]

DORF Accuracy Percent: ________ %

100 x (Words Correct / Words Correct + Errors)

Accuracy Value from Table = ____________________ [3]

DIBELS Composite Score (add values 1–3) = [ ]

If DORF is below 40 and Retell is not administered, use 0 for the Retell value only for calculating the DIBELS Composite Score. Do not calculate the composite score if any of the values are missing.

End of Year Benchmark

DORF Words Correct = ____________________ [1]

Retell Score __________ **x 2** = ____________________ [2]

DORF Accuracy Percent: ________ %

100 x (Words Correct / Words Correct + Errors)

Accuracy Value from Table = ____________________ [3]

DIBELS Composite Score (add values 1–3) = [ ]

If DORF is below 40 and Retell is not administered, use 0 for the Retell value only for calculating the DIBELS Composite Score. Do not calculate the composite score if any of the values are missing.

3 Third Grade DIBELS® Next Composite Score Worksheet

© Dynamic Measurement Group, Inc. / August 31, 2010

The *DIBELS* Composite Score is used to interpret student results for *DIBELS Next.* Most data-management services will calculate the composite score for you. If you do not use a data-management service or if your data-management service does not calculate it, you can use this worksheet to calculate the composite score.

Name: ______________________ **Class:** ______________________

Beginning, Middle, and End of Year	
DORF Accuracy Percent	Accuracy Value
0% – 85%	0
86%	8
87%	16
88%	24
89%	32
90%	40
91%	48
92%	56
93%	64
94%	72
95%	80
96%	88
97%	96
98%	104
99%	112
100%	120

Beginning of Year Benchmark

DORF Words Correct = ______________ [1]

Retell Score __________ **x 2** = ______________ [2]

Daze Adjusted Score __________ **x 4** = ______________ [3]

DORF Accuracy Percent: ________ %
100 x (Words Correct / Words Correct + Errors)

Accuracy Value from Table = ______________ [4]

DIBELS Composite Score (add values 1–4) = [ ]

If DORF is below 40 and Retell is not administered, use 0 for the Retell value only for calculating the DIBELS Composite Score. Do not calculate the composite score if any of the values are missing.

Middle of Year Benchmark

DORF Words Correct = ______________ [1]

Retell Score __________ **x 2** = ______________ [2]

Daze Adjusted Score __________ **x 4** = ______________ [3]

DORF Accuracy Percent: ________ %
100 x (Words Correct / Words Correct + Errors)

Accuracy Value from Table = ______________ [4]

DIBELS Composite Score (add values 1–4) = [ ]

If DORF is below 40 and Retell is not administered, use 0 for the Retell value only for calculating the DIBELS Composite Score. Do not calculate the composite score if any of the values are missing.

End of Year Benchmark

DORF Words Correct = ______________ [1]

Retell Score __________ **x 2** = ______________ [2]

Daze Adjusted Score __________ **x 4** = ______________ [3]

DORF Accuracy Percent: ________ %
100 x (Words Correct / Words Correct + Errors)

Accuracy Value from Table = ______________ [4]

DIBELS Composite Score (add values 1–4) = [ ]

If DORF is below 40 and Retell is not administered, use 0 for the Retell value only for calculating the DIBELS Composite Score. Do not calculate the composite score if any of the values are missing.

4 Fourth Grade DIBELS® Next Composite Score Worksheet

The *DIBELS* Composite Score is used to interpret student results for *DIBELS Next*. Most data-management services will calculate the composite score for you. If you do not use a data-management service or if your data-management service does not calculate it, you can use this worksheet to calculate the composite score.

Name: ______________________ **Class:** ______________________

Beginning, Middle, and End of Year	
DORF Accuracy Percent	Accuracy Value
0% – 85%	0
86%	8
87%	16
88%	24
89%	32
90%	40
91%	48
92%	56
93%	64
94%	72
95%	80
96%	88
97%	96
98%	104
99%	112
100%	120

Beginning of Year Benchmark

DORF Words Correct = ______________ [1]

Retell Score ________ **x 2** = ______________ [2]

Daze Adjusted Score ________ **x 4** = ______________ [3]

DORF Accuracy Percent: ________ %
100 x (Words Correct / Words Correct + Errors)

Accuracy Value from Table = ______________ [4]

DIBELS Composite Score (add values 1–4) = [ ]

If DORF is below 40 and Retell is not administered, use 0 for the Retell value only for calculating the DIBELS Composite Score. Do not calculate the composite score if any of the values are missing.

Middle of Year Benchmark

DORF Words Correct = ______________ [1]

Retell Score ________ **x 2** = ______________ [2]

Daze Adjusted Score ________ **x 4** = ______________ [3]

DORF Accuracy Percent: ________ %
100 x (Words Correct / Words Correct + Errors)

Accuracy Value from Table = ______________ [4]

DIBELS Composite Score (add values 1–4) = [ ]

If DORF is below 40 and Retell is not administered, use 0 for the Retell value only for calculating the DIBELS Composite Score. Do not calculate the composite score if any of the values are missing.

End of Year Benchmark

DORF Words Correct = ______________ [1]

Retell Score ________ **x 2** = ______________ [2]

Daze Adjusted Score ________ **x 4** = ______________ [3]

DORF Accuracy Percent: ________ %
100 x (Words Correct / Words Correct + Errors)

Accuracy Value from Table = ______________ [4]

DIBELS Composite Score (add values 1–4) = [ ]

If DORF is below 40 and Retell is not administered, use 0 for the Retell value only for calculating the DIBELS Composite Score. Do not calculate the composite score if any of the values are missing.

5 Fifth Grade DIBELS® Next Composite Score Worksheet

© Dynamic Measurement Group, Inc. / August 31, 2010

The *DIBELS* Composite Score is used to interpret student results for *DIBELS Next*. Most data-management services will calculate the composite score for you. If you do not use a data-management service or if your data-management service does not calculate it, you can use this worksheet to calculate the composite score.

Name: ______________________ **Class:** ______________________

Beginning, Middle, and End of Year	
DORF Accuracy Percent	Accuracy Value
0% – 85%	0
86%	8
87%	16
88%	24
89%	32
90%	40
91%	48
92%	56
93%	64
94%	72
95%	80
96%	88
97%	96
98%	104
99%	112
100%	120

Beginning of Year Benchmark

DORF Words Correct = __________ [1]

Retell Score __________ **x 2** = __________ [2]

Daze Adjusted Score __________ **x 4** = __________ [3]

DORF Accuracy Percent: ________ %
100 x (Words Correct / Words Correct + Errors)

Accuracy Value from Table = __________ [4]

DIBELS Composite Score (add values 1–4) = ☐

If DORF is below 40 and Retell is not administered, use 0 for the Retell value only for calculating the DIBELS Composite Score. Do not calculate the composite score if any of the values are missing.

Middle of Year Benchmark

DORF Words Correct = __________ [1]

Retell Score __________ **x 2** = __________ [2]

Daze Adjusted Score __________ **x 4** = __________ [3]

DORF Accuracy Percent: ________ %
100 x (Words Correct / Words Correct + Errors)

Accuracy Value from Table = __________ [4]

DIBELS Composite Score (add values 1–4) = ☐

If DORF is below 40 and Retell is not administered, use 0 for the Retell value only for calculating the DIBELS Composite Score. Do not calculate the composite score if any of the values are missing.

End of Year Benchmark

DORF Words Correct = __________ [1]

Retell Score __________ **x 2** = __________ [2]

Daze Adjusted Score __________ **x 4** = __________ [3]

DORF Accuracy Percent: ________ %
100 x (Words Correct / Words Correct + Errors)

Accuracy Value from Table = __________ [4]

DIBELS Composite Score (add values 1–4) = ☐

If DORF is below 40 and Retell is not administered, use 0 for the Retell value only for calculating the DIBELS Composite Score. Do not calculate the composite score if any of the values are missing.

6 Sixth Grade DIBELS® Next Composite Score Worksheet

© Dynamic Measurement Group, Inc. / August 31, 2010

The *DIBELS* Composite Score is used to interpret student results for *DIBELS Next*. Most data-management services will calculate the composite score for you. If you do not use a data-management service or if your data-management service does not calculate it, you can use this worksheet to calculate the composite score.

Name: ______________________ **Class:** ______________________

Beginning, Middle, and End of Year	
DORF Accuracy Percent	Accuracy Value
0% – 85%	0
86%	8
87%	16
88%	24
89%	32
90%	40
91%	48
92%	56
93%	64
94%	72
95%	80
96%	88
97%	96
98%	104
99%	112
100%	120

Beginning of Year Benchmark

DORF Words Correct = ______________ [1]

Retell Score ________ **x 2** = ______________ [2]

Daze Adjusted Score ________ **x 4** = ______________ [3]

DORF Accuracy Percent: ________ %
100 x (Words Correct / Words Correct + Errors)

Accuracy Value from Table = ______________ [4]

DIBELS Composite Score (add values 1–4) = ☐

If DORF is below 40 and Retell is not administered, use 0 for the Retell value only for calculating the DIBELS Composite Score. Do not calculate the composite score if any of the values are missing.

Middle of Year Benchmark

DORF Words Correct = ______________ [1]

Retell Score ________ **x 2** = ______________ [2]

Daze Adjusted Score ________ **x 4** = ______________ [3]

DORF Accuracy Percent: ________ %
100 x (Words Correct / Words Correct + Errors)

Accuracy Value from Table = ______________ [4]

DIBELS Composite Score (add values 1–4) = ☐

If DORF is below 40 and Retell is not administered, use 0 for the Retell value only for calculating the DIBELS Composite Score. Do not calculate the composite score if any of the values are missing.

End of Year Benchmark

DORF Words Correct = ______________ [1]

Retell Score ________ **x 2** = ______________ [2]

Daze Adjusted Score ________ **x 4** = ______________ [3]

DORF Accuracy Percent: ________ %
100 x (Words Correct / Words Correct + Errors)

Accuracy Value from Table = ______________ [4]

DIBELS Composite Score (add values 1–4) = ☐

If DORF is below 40 and Retell is not administered, use 0 for the Retell value only for calculating the DIBELS Composite Score. Do not calculate the composite score if any of the values are missing.

Bibliography

Adams, M. J. (1990). *Beginning to read: Thinking and learning about print.* Cambridge, MA: MIT Press.

Buck, J., & Torgesen, J. (2003). *The relationship between performance on a measure of Oral Reading Fluency and performance on the Florida Comprehensive Assessment Test.* (FCRR Technical Report #1) Tallahassee, FL: Florida Center for Reading Research.

Catts, H. W., & Kahmi, A. G. (1999). *Language and reading disabilities.* Needham Heights, MA: Allyn & Bacon.

Chiappe, P. R., Siegel, L.S., & Wade-Woolley, L. (2002). Linguistic diversity and the development of reading skills: A longitudinal study. *Scientific Studies of Reading, 6,* 369–400. doi:10.1207/S1532799XSSR0604_04

Crowder, R., & Wagner, R. (1992). *The psychology of reading: An introduction.* New York: Oxford Press.

Deno, S. L. (1985). Curriculum-based measurement: The emerging alternative. *Exceptional Children, 52*(3), 219–232.

Deno, S. L. (1989). Curriculum-based measurement and special education services: A fundamental and direct relationship. In M. R. Shinn (Ed.), *Curriculum-based measurement: Assessing special children* (pp. 1–17). New York: Guilford Press.

Deno, S. L., & Fuchs, L. S. (1987). Developing curriculum-based measurement systems for data-based special education problem solving. *Focus on Exceptional Children, 19*(8), 1–16.

Deno, S. L., & Mirkin, P. K. (1977). *Data-based program modification: A manual.* Reston, VA: Council for Exceptional Children.

Dewitz, P., & Dewitz, P. K. (2003). They can read the words, but they can't understand: Refining comprehension assessment. *Reading Teacher, 56,* 422–435.

Dowhower, S. L. (1991). Speaking of prosody: Fluency's unattended bedfellow. *Theory Into Practice, 30,* 165–175. doi:10.1080/00405849109543497

Duke, N. K., Pressley, M., & Hilden, K. (2004). Difficulties with reading comprehension. In C. A. Stone, E. R. Silliman, B. J. Ehren, & K. Apel (Eds.), *Handbook of language and literacy* (pp. 501–520). New York: Guilford Press.

Ehri, L. C. (1991). Development of the ability to read words. In R. Barr, M. Kamil, P. Mosenthal & P. Pearson (Eds.), *Handbook of reading research* (Vol. 2, pp. 383–417). New York: Longman.

Ehri, L. C. (1998). Grapheme-phoneme knowledge is essential for learning to read words in English. In J. L. Metsala, & L. C. Ehri (Eds.), *Word recognition in beginning literacy* (pp. 3–40). Mahwah, NJ: Erlbaum.

Ehri, L. C. (2002). Phases of acquisition in learning to read words and implications for teaching. In R. Stainthorp & P. Tomlinson (Eds.), *Learning and teaching reading* (pp. 7–28). London: British Journal of Educational Psychology Monograph Series II.

Ehri, L. C. (2004). Teaching phonemic awareness and phonics: An explanation of the National Reading Panel meta-analyses. In P. McCardle & V. Chhabra (Eds.), *The voice of evidence in reading research.* Baltimore: Brookes.

Fuchs, D., & Fuchs, L.S. (2006). Introduction to responsiveness-to-intervention: What, why, and how valid is it? *Reading Research Quarterly, 41,* 92–99. doi:10.1598/RRQ.41.1.4

Fuchs, L. S., & Deno, S. L. (1991). Paradigmatic distinctions between instructionally relevant measurement models. *Exceptional Children, 57*(6), 488–500.

Geva, E., Yaghoub-Zadeh, Z., & Schuster, B. (2000). Understanding individual differences in word recognition skills of ESL children. *Annals of Dyslexia, 50*(1), 121–154. doi:10.1007/s11881-000-0020-8

Gillon, G. T. (2004). *Phonological awareness: From research to practice.* New York: Guilford Press.

Goldman, S. R., & Rakestraw, J. A. (2000). Structural aspects of constructing meaning from text. In M. Kamil, P. Mosenthal, P. D. Pearson, & R. Barr (Eds.), *Handbook of reading research* (Vol. III, pp. 311–336). Mahwah, NJ: Erlbaum.

Good, R. H., & Kaminski, R. A. (1996). Assessment for instructional decisions: Toward a proactive/prevention model of decision making for early literacy skills. *School Psychology Quarterly, 11,* 326–336. doi:10.1037/h0088938

Haager, D., & Windmueller, M. P. (2001). Early reading intervention for English language learners at-risk for learning disabilities: Student and teacher outcomes in an urban school. *Learning Disability Quarterly, 24*(4), 235–250. doi:10.2307/1511113

Kame'enui, E. J., Carnine, D. W., Dixon, R. C., Simmons, D. C., & Coyne, M. D. (2002). *Effective teaching strategies that accommodate diverse learners* (2nd ed.). Upper Saddle River, NJ: Merrill Prentice Hall.

Kaminski, R. A., & Cummings, K. D. (2007, Winter). Assessment for learning: Using general outcomes measures. *Threshold*, 26–28.

Kaminski, R. A., & Good, R. H., III. (1996). Toward a technology for assessing basic early literacy skills. *School Psychology Review 25*, 215–227.

Kaminski, R. A., & Good, R. H., III. (1998). Assessing early literacy skills in a problem-solving model: Dynamic Indicators of Basic Early Literacy Skills. In M. R. Shinn (Ed.), *Advanced applications of curriculum-based measurement* (pp. 113–142). New York: Guilford Press.

LaBerge, D., & Samuels, S. (1974). Toward a theory of automatic information processing in reading. *Cognitive Psychology, 6,* 293–323. doi:10.1016/0010-0285(74)90015-2

Lesaux, N. K., & Siegel, L. S. (2003). The development of reading in children who speak English as a second language. *Developmental Psychology, 39*, 1005–1019. doi:10.1037/0012-1649.39.6.1005

Leybaert, J., & Charlier, B. (1996). The effect of exposure to phonetically augmented lipspeech in the prelingual deaf. In R. Campbell, B. Dodd, & D. Burnham (Eds.) *Hearing by eye II: Advances in the psychology of speechreading and auditory-visual speech* (pp. 283–301). Hove, England: Taylor & Francis.

Liberman, I., & Liberman, A. (1990). Whole language vs. code emphasis: Underlying assumptions and their implications for reading instruction. *Annals of Dyslexia, 40*, 51–76. doi:10.1007/BF02648140

Logan, G. D. (1988). Toward an instance theory of automatization. *Psychology Review, 95,* 492–527. doi:10.1037/0033-295X.95.4.492

McGuinness, D. (1997). *Why our children can't read–and what we can do about it: A scientific revolution in reading.* New York: Touchstone.

McGuinness, D. (2005). *Language development and learning to read: The scientific study of how language development affects reading skill.* Cambridge, MA: MIT Press.

Moores, D. (1996). *Educating the deaf: Psychology, principles, and practices* (4th ed.). Boston: Houghton Mifflin.

National Reading Panel. (2000). *Teaching children to read: An evidence-based assessment of the scientific research literature on reading and its implications for reading instruction.* Reports of the subgroups. Washington, DC: National Institute of Child Health and Human Development.

National Research Council. (1998). *Preventing reading difficulties in young children.* Washington, DC: National Academy Press.

Paul, R. (2001). *Language disorders from infancy through adolescence: Assessment and intervention.* St. Louis, MO: Mosby, Inc.

Perfetti, C. (1985). *Reading ability.* New York: Oxford Press.

Pikulski, J. J., & Chard, D. J. (2005). Fluency: Bridge between decoding and reading comprehension. *The Reading Teacher, 58*(6), 510–519. doi:10.1598/RT.58.6.2

Pressley, M. (2000). What should comprehension instruction be the instruction of? In M. Kamil, P. Mosenthal, P. D. Pearson, & R. Barr (Eds.), *Handbook of reading research* (Vol. III, pp. 545–562). Mahwah, NJ: Erlbaum.

Rathvon, N. (2004). *Early reading assessment: A practitioner's handbook.* New York: Guilford.

Scarborough, H. S. (1998). Early identification of children at risk for reading disabilities: Phonological awareness and some other promising predictors. In B.K. Shapiro, P. J. Accardo, & A. J. Capute (Eds.), *Specific reading disability: A view of the spectrum* (pp. 75–119). Baltimore: York Press.

Schreiber, P. A. (1987). Prosody and structure in children's syntactic processing. In R. Horowitz & S. J. Samuels (Eds.), *Comprehending oral and written language* (pp. 243–270). New York: Academic Press.

Schreiber, P. A. (1991). Understanding prosody's role in reading acquisition. *Theory Into Practice, 30,* 158–164. doi:10.1080/00405849109543496

Share, D. L. (1995). Phonological recoding and self-teaching: *Sine qua non* of reading acquisition. *Cognition, 55,* 151–218. doi:10.1016/0010-0277(94)00645-2

Share, D. L., & Stanovich, K. E. (1995). Cognitive processes in early reading development: Accommodating individual differences into a model of acquisition. *Issues in Education: Contributions from Educational Psychology, 1,* 1–57.

Shinn, M. R. (1995). Best practices in using curriculum-based measurement in a problem-solving model. In J. G. A. Thomas (Ed.), *Best practices in school psychology III* (Vol. 3, pp. 671–697). Silver Springs, MD: National Association of School Psychologists.

Simmons, D. C., & Kame'enui, E. J. (Eds.). (1998). *What reading research tells us about children with diverse learning needs: Bases and basics.* Mahwah, NJ: Lawrence Erlbaum Associates, Inc.

Stahl, S. A., & Fairbanks, M. M. (1986). The effects of vocabulary instruction: A model-based meta-analysis. *Review of Educational Research, 56*(1), 72–110.

Stahl, S. A., & Murray, B. A. (1994). Defining phonological awareness and its relationship to early reading. *Journal of Educational Psychology, 82*, 221–234. doi:10.1037/0022-0663.86.2.221

Stahl, S. A., & Murray, B.A. (2006). Defining phonological awareness and its relationship to early reading. In K.A.D. Stahl & M.C. McKenna (Eds.), *Reading research at work: Foundations of effective practice* (pp. 92–113). New York: Guilford Press.

Tilly, W. D., III. (2008). The evolution of school psychology to science-based practice. In A. Thomas & J. Grimes (Eds.), *Best practices in school psychology V* (pp. 18–32). Washington, DC: National Association of School Psychologists.

Torgesen, J. K., Wagner, R. K., Rashotte, C.A., Rose, E., Lindamood, P., Conway, T., et al. (1999). Preventing reading failure in young children with phonological processing disabilities: Group and individual responses to instruction. *Journal of Educational Psychology, 91,* 579–593. doi:10.1037/0022-0663.91.4.579

Troia, G. A. (2004). Building word recognition skills through empirically validated instructional practices. In E. R. Silliman & L. C. Wilkinson (Eds.), *Language and literacy learning in schools* (pp. 98–129). New York: Guilford Press.

Wagner, R. K., Torgesen, J. K., & Rashotte, C. A. (1994). The development of reading-related phonological processing abilities: New evidence of bi-directional causality from a latent variable longitudinal study. *Developmental Psychology, 30*, 73–78. doi:10.1037/0012-1649.30.1.73

Williams, K. T. (2001). *Group reading assessment and diagnostic evaluation (GRADE).* New York: Pearson.

Wilson, J. (2005). *The relationship of Dynamic Indicators of Basic Early Literacy Skills (DIBELS) Oral Reading Fluency to performance on Arizona Instrument to Measure Standards (AIMS).* Tempe, AZ: Tempe School District No. 3.

Wolf, M., & Katzir-Cohen, T. (2001). Reading fluency and its intervention. *Scientific Studies of Reading, 5,* 211–238. doi:10.1207/S1532799XSSR0503_2

Yopp, H. K. (1988). The validity and reliability of phonemic awareness tests. *Reading Research Quarterly, 23*(2), 159–177. doi:10.2307/747800